The Urbana Free Library

To renew materials call
217-367-4057

2-06

	DATE DUE		
FEB 24 2006			
APR 01 2006			

ARBITRARY BORDERS

Political Boundaries in World History

The Division of the Middle East
The Treaty of Sèvres

The Iron Curtain
The Cold War in Europe

The Mason–Dixon Line

Vietnam: The 17th Parallel

Korea: The 38th Parallel

The U.S.–Mexico Border
The Treaty of Guadalupe Hidalgo

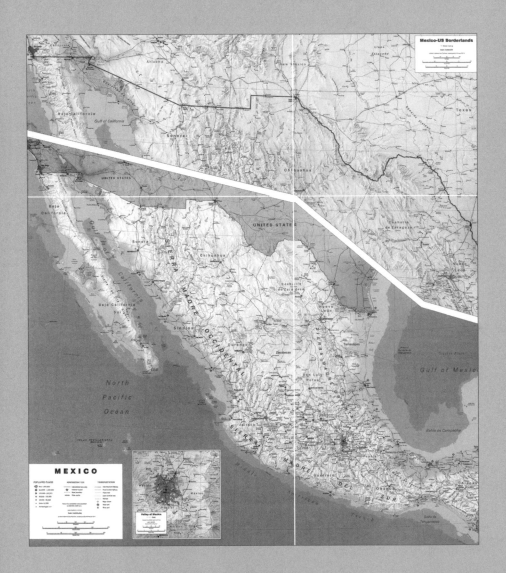

ARBITRARY BORDERS

Political Boundaries in World History

The U.S.-Mexico Border
The Treaty of Guadalupe Hidalgo

John C. Davenport

Foreword by
Senator George J. Mitchell

Introduction by
James I. Matray
California State University, Chico

CHELSEA HOUSE
PUBLISHERS
A Haights Cross Communications Company

Philadelphia

2-06
35⁰⁰

FRONTIS   Map of the border between the United States and Mexico and the surrounding territory.

.

CHELSEA HOUSE PUBLISHERS

VP, NEW PRODUCT DEVELOPMENT   Sally Cheney
DIRECTOR OF PRODUCTION   Kim Shinners
CREATIVE MANAGER   Takeshi Takahashi
MANUFACTURING MANAGER   Diann Grasse

Staff for THE U.S.–MEXICO BORDER

EXECUTIVE EDITOR   Lee Marcott
PRODUCTION EDITOR   Megan Emery
ASSOCIATE PHOTO EDITOR   Noelle Nardone
SERIES DESIGNER   Keith Trego
COVER DESIGNER   Keith Trego
LAYOUT   EJB Publishing Services

A Haights Cross Communications ✦ Company

www.chelseahouse.com

First Printing

9 8 7 6 5 4 3 2 1

Library of Congress Cataloging-in-Publication Data
Davenport, John, 1960–
     The U.S.-Mexico border / by John Davenport
          p. cm. — (Arbitrary borders)
     Includes biobliographical references
     ISBN 0-7910-7833-7
  1. Mexican-American Border Region—History. 2. Mexico—Relations—
United States. 3. United States—Relations—Mexico. I. Title: United
States-Mexico border. II. Title. III. Series.
     F786.D375 2004
     972'.1—dc22
                                              2004003391

Contents

Foreword

Senator **George J. Mitchell**

I spent years working for peace in Northern Ireland and in the Middle East. I also made many visits to the Balkans during the long and violent conflict there.

Each of the three areas is unique; so is each conflict. But there are also some similarities: in each, there are differences over religion, national identity, and territory.

Deep religious differences that lead to murderous hostility are common in human history. Competing aspirations involving national identity are more recent occurrences, but often have been just as deadly.

Territorial disputes—two or more people claiming the same land—are as old as humankind. Almost without exception, such disputes have been a factor in recent conflicts. It is impossible to calculate the extent to which the demand for land—as opposed to religion, national identity, or other factors— figures in the motivation of people caught up in conflict. In my experience it is a substantial factor that has played a role in each of the three conflicts mentioned above.

In Northern Ireland and the Middle East, the location of the border was a major factor in igniting and sustaining the conflict. And it is memorialized in a dramatic and visible way: through the construction of large walls whose purpose is to physically separate the two communities.

In Belfast, the capital and largest city in Northern Ireland, the so-called "Peace Line" cuts through the heart of the city, right across urban streets. Up to thirty feet high in places, topped with barbed wire in others, it is an ugly reminder of the duration and intensity of the conflict.

In the Middle East, as I write these words, the government of Israel has embarked on a huge and controversial effort to construct a security fence roughly along the line that separates Israel from the West Bank.

Having served a tour of duty with the U.S. Army in Berlin, which was once the site of the best known of modern walls, I am skeptical of their long-term value, although they often serve short-term needs. But it cannot be said that such structures represent a new idea. Ancient China built the Great Wall to deter nomadic Mongol tribes from attacking its population.

In much the same way, other early societies established boundaries and fortified them militarily to achieve the goal of self-protection. Borders always have separated people. Indeed, that is their purpose.

This series of books examines the important and timely issue of the significance of arbitrary borders in history. Each volume focuses attention on a territorial division, but the analytical approach is more comprehensive. These studies describe arbitrary borders as places where people interact differently from the way they would if the boundary did not exist. This pattern is especially pronounced where there is no geographic reason for the boundary and no history recognizing its legitimacy. Even though many borders have been defined without legal precision, governments frequently have provided vigorous monitoring and military defense for them.

This series will show how the migration of people and exchange of goods almost always work to undermine the separation that borders seek to maintain. The continuing evolution of a European community provides a contemporary example illustrating this point, most obviously with the adoption of a single currency. Moreover, even former Soviet bloc nations have eliminated barriers to economic and political integration.

Globalization has emerged as one of the most powerful forces in international affairs during the twenty-first century. Not only have markets for the exchange of goods and services become genuinely worldwide, but instant communication and sharing of information have shattered old barriers separating people. Some scholars even argue that globalization has made the entire concept of a territorial nation-state irrelevant. Although the assertion is certainly premature and probably wrong, it highlights the importance of recognizing how borders often have reflected and affirmed the cultural, ethnic, or linguistic perimeters that define a people or a country.

Since the Cold War ended, competition over resources or a variety of interests threaten boundaries more than ever, resulting in contentious interaction, conflict, adaptation, and intermixture. How people define their borders is also a factor in determining how events develop in the surrounding region. This series will provide detailed descriptions of selected arbitrary borders in history with the objective of providing insights on how artificial boundaries separating people will influence international affairs during the next century.

Senator George J. Mitchell
October 2003

Introduction

James I. Matray
California State University, Chico

Throughout history, borders have separated people. Scholars have devoted considerable attention to assessing the significance and impact of territorial boundaries on the course of human history, explaining how they often have been sources of controversy and conflict. In the modern age, the rise of nation-states in Europe created the need for governments to negotiate treaties to confirm boundary lines that periodically changed as a consequence of wars and revolutions. European expansion in the nineteenth century imposed new borders on Africa and Asia. Many native peoples viewed these boundaries as arbitrary and, after independence, continued to contest their legitimacy. At the end of both world wars in the twentieth century, world leaders drew artificial and impermanent lines separating assorted people around the globe. Borders certainly are among the most important factors that have influenced the development of world affairs.

Chelsea House Publishers decided to publish a collection of books looking at arbitrary borders in history in response to the revival of the nuclear crisis in North Korea in October 2002. Recent tensions on the Korean peninsula are a direct consequence of the partitioning of Korea at the 38th parallel after World War II. Other nations in the course of human history have suffered due to similar artificial divisions. The reasons for establishing arbitrary borders have differed, but usually arise from either domestic or international factors and are often a combination of both. In the case of Korea, it was the United States and the Soviet Union who decided in August 1945 to partition the country at the 38th parallel. Ostensibly, the purpose was to facilitate the acceptance of the surrender of Japanese forces at the end of World War II. However, historians have presented persuasive evidence that a political contest existed inside Korea to decide the future of the nation after forty years of Japanese colonial rule. Therefore, Korea's division at the 38th parallel was an artificial boundary that symbolized the split among the Korean people about the nation's destiny. On the right were conservative landowners who had closely aligned with the Japanese, many of whom were outright collaborators. On the left, there were far more individuals who favored revolutionary change. In fact, Communists provided the leadership and direction for the independence movement inside Korea from the 1920s until the end of World War II. After 1945, two Koreas emerged that reflected these divergent ideologies. But the Korean people have never accepted the legitimacy or permanence of the division imposed by foreign powers.

Korea's experience in dealing with the artificial division of its country may well be unique, but it is not without historical parallels. The first set of books in this series on arbitrary borders examines six key chapters in human history. One volume will look at the history of the 38th parallel in Korea. Other volumes will provide description and analysis of the division of the Middle East after World War I; the Cold War as symbolized by the Iron Curtain in Central Europe; the United States.-Mexico Border; the 17th parallel in Vietnam, and the Mason-Dixon Line. Future books will address the Great Wall in China, Northern Ireland's border, and the Green Line in Israel. Admittedly, there are many significant differences between these boundaries, but these books will cover as many common themes as possible. In so doing, each will help readers conceptualize how factors such as colonialism, culture, and economics determine the nature of contact between people along these borders. Although globalization has emerged as a powerful force working against the creation and maintenance of lines separating people, boundaries are not likely to disappear as factors with a continuing influence on world events. This series of books will provide insights about the impact of arbitrary borders on human history and how such borders continue to shape the modern world.

James I. Matray
Chico, California
November 2003

1

One Day
on the Border

As the ink dried on the paper, the diplomats congratulated themselves. They had ended a war, restructured relations throughout the hemisphere, and drawn a new border between the United States and the Mexican Republic. Reveling in the warm winter breezes of central Mexico, the American representatives stood back from the document they had just signed and took it all in. The old West, from Texas to California, now belonged solely to them. In one fell swoop, the United States had become a continental nation; it truly did stretch from sea to shining sea.

The Mexican signatories also considered themselves fortunate. They had surrendered fully half of their nation's landmass to the voracious northerners. Still, despite the best efforts of their adversaries to swallow the country whole, Mexico remained intact, independent, and sovereign. For vastly different reasons, both negotiating teams could claim victory in one sense or another. Satisfied with the outcome of their meeting, the Mexican and American representatives left the town of Guadalupe Hidalgo bound for their respective capitals, planning to present the freshly completed treaty to skeptical legislators. Exhausted but content that they had wrung the best possible deal from their opponents, none of those who had labored to perfect the Treaty of Guadalupe Hidalgo in 1848 could have imagined how their piece of paper might tragically alter the life of an innocent young man named Esequiel Hernandez more than 150 years later.

Esequiel Hernandez was a child of the border. Born and raised in the United States, but within a stone's throw of Mexico, he knew what it felt like to hover tenuously between two worlds, between two realities, part of both but bound to a community that spanned arbitrary lines drawn in faraway national centers of power. For this young man, as with many hundreds of thousands more people who call the U.S.-Mexican border "home," a balance had to be struck between identities. He was part Mexican, part American, but all border. This 2,000-mile stretch of land was his home, a place of special meaning.

On May 20, 1997, as was his custom after school, the 18-year-old Hernandez was tending his family's herd of goats as they grazed slowly along the dusty hillsides, nibbling at the sparse greenery that punctuated the countryside around Redford, Texas. Not far from where the boy maintained his vigil, the Rio Grande rolled languidly toward the Gulf of Mexico. Down its center ran the official boundary line between the United States and Mexico, a border drawn by politicians who had never known and would never experience the sensation of living daily in a transitional space, a tightly circumscribed area where cultures and people merged into a vibrant whole. Where the politicians saw only difference and divergence, a community emerged that took convergence and interdependence for granted. Conflict periodically roiled the community, to be sure, but it was a mutually destructive yet almost familial contest among people competing for scant resources that they shared only reluctantly. The tension that broke into deadly violence on this spring day was of another kind; it blew in from the outside like the warm wind that wafted over the young goatherd.

On a map, Hernandez stood on the U.S.-Mexican border, but to him all the scrub-choked ground looked the same, regardless of which side of the river it lay on. The landscape for this young man formed an unbroken and unblemished whole. The boundary line that meant so much to politicians in Washington, D.C., and Mexico City was invisible to him. This was his home, his place in the world. What went through the teenager's mind as his goats wandered around had nothing to do with international relations or territorial integrity. He had a driver's license test coming up, and college, where he hoped to study for a career in the park service. That, though, was tomorrow. Today, there were the goats. In order to protect his animals, Hernandez always carried an old .22-caliber rifle.

Not far from Esequiel Hernandez's herd, other eyes surveyed the terrain. Those belonged to a four-soldier U.S. Marine patrol that had traveled all the way from Camp Pendleton, in California, to take part in operations conducted by Joint Task

Force Six, a collaborative effort between the United States military and the Border Patrol aimed at stopping drug smugglers from slipping into the United States from Mexico with their deadly merchandise.

The Marines were tense. Law enforcement fell outside of their normal range of duties: They had been trained to storm enemy beaches, not to guard borders. The patrol that scoured this small patch of Texas was composed of fighters, not police officers. Yet as Marines, the troops followed orders, so here they were, moving stealthily through the brush—in full camouflage and carrying automatic rifles. Scanning the horizon, they kept reminding themselves that drug smugglers often employed boys as scouts to make sure an area was clear of Border Patrol agents before entering it. These scouts, the Marines recalled, almost always carried guns.

As evening came and the sun began to set along the border, the hidden Marines pushed forward. About 500 feet ahead of them, Hernandez thought he saw a coyote, or perhaps it was a rustler out to steal his goats. The boy kept a sharp lookout for "people coming from Mexico messing with my goats."[1] Taking no chances, he raised his antique rifle and fired a single round. Hearing the hollow pop of small arms, the Marines immediately sought out the source. They crept up on Hernandez, moving "bush to bush," following him for a seeming eternity of 20 minutes. After having maintained a "visual observation" of the goatherd, the patrol assumed an "immediate defensive posture,"[2] and prepared for action. Suddenly, a second shot rang out, and the teenager fell to the ground, mortally wounded by a bullet from one of the Marines' M16s.

At precisely 6:27 P.M., the Marines coolly reported over their radio that they had a "man down."[3] Even though one of the team's members was a combat medic, no one tended to Hernandez's wound. The teenager lay bleeding on the hard Texas ground for half an hour. As the warm sun moved languidly toward the western horizon and the Rio Grande meandered along its ancient course to the Gulf of Mexico, Esequiel

Hernandez slowly died. His short life came to an end because another American mistook him for a Mexican crossing an imaginary line. Fear, suspicion, ethnic stereotypes, and a border consisting of dots and dashes on a map cost one young Texan his life.

Like most who live and interact daily along the border, Hernandez saw no clear boundary between "us" and "them" in the muddy waters of the Rio Grande. The border was little more than a vague directional marker, one referred to while moving from one part of a seamless whole to another. Unlike the Marines who took his life, the boy saw no frontier to be defended, no line to be held against the "foreign" Mexicans across the river. Esequiel Hernandez's reality encompassed a single place—960,000 square miles that is known as MexAmerica to some, *la frontera* to others, and simply "the border" to most of its inhabitants.[4] It occupies a rare space, a broad landscape existing as much in the imagination as in the mountains, deserts, and rivers that lend the region its beauty and majesty. The border is a place where a unique community flourishes, animated by "common daily activity ... shared natural resources ... and labor markets that overlap the political boundary."[5] It is a single community, a coherent "transnational settlement space"—and an arbitrary border cuts it in half.

The U.S.-Mexico borderlands embrace and nourish a diverse human population within which one can perceive clearly what the sociologist Pablo Vila called "the complex process of identity construction,"[6] so crucial to understanding why the Marines imagined an unassailable international border where Esequiel Hernandez saw only grass for his goats to graze and brush for them to browse. Where they saw division, he observed the unity of history and place and an effervescent regional community replete with points of conflict and opportunities for cooperation. Border folk eye one another warily and rarely agree on much despite a powerful interdependence that at times comes close to resembling symbiosis. Yet for all of the ambivalence, the agreements and disagreements, the issues being debated along the border remain stubbornly incomprehensible to

day in 1997 is the latest chapter of a story that begins with that single piece of paper drawn up and signed in a small Mexican town in the middle of the nineteenth century.

2

The Edge
of Empire

Long before the Treaty of Guadalupe Hidalgo created an arbitrary border down the middle of perhaps the most vibrant and dynamic region in the Americas, the area that is now the American Southwest and the Mexican far north existed as a frontier in the truest sense of the word. It represented a transitional space that stood at the farthest reaches of the sixteenth-century Spanish Empire in the New World. A huge expanse of mostly arid land, *la frontera* marked the point at which European settlement blended into the much older world of Native America. Even at this early date, the border functioned more as a bridge than a wall, a place where people and cultures gave to and took from one another. Characterized by cautious, often reluctant interaction broken by periods of intense conflict, the frontier experience represented an ongoing human process of discovery and community formation.

This gradual evolution, difficult under the best circumstances, faced derailment by numerous obstacles, not the least of which was the forbidding natural environment that served as its venue. A sizable portion of the frontier baked in temperatures that routinely reached 140° F. Scorching winds desiccated (dried out) the soil and churned up huge, blinding dust storms. Annual average rainfall of a mere eight inches barely moistened the parched ground. Flat for the most part, the region absorbed the scant precipitation like a massive sponge. Only rarely was the landscape crossed by the life-giving waters of rivers such as the roaring Colorado, which twisted along its path through sheer cliffs; the shallow, turbid Gila and Salt rivers; and the Great River—the Rio Grande—which meandered for hundreds of miles before spilling into the Gulf of Mexico.

Throughout the region, brooding mountain ranges of up to 9,000 feet in elevation and desolate sinks limited human habitation to those Native Americans hardy enough to sustain themselves on the area's scant vegetation and meager animal resources. Such groups lived precarious (dangerous) existences, roaming the land in small hunter-gatherer bands or uniting into scattered communities of farmers, who scratched out a living from the hard ground. Altogether, Native Americans speaking six different languages lived in the future border region, no group connected to the others except by the loosest bonds of shared hardship. Where sufficient water offered itself for human use, Native American villages sprang up, and their residents grew beans, corn, and squash as staple crops. On the margins of the Great River, such settlements formed and successfully exploited the dependable water that flowed out of the northern mountains. Eventually, 40,000 Native Americans set about tilling the soil on both shores of what would become the U.S.-Mexican border.

The Rio Grande, however, was still just a river, and the deserts still deserts. Together, these topographic realities meant little in terms of regional community. Native Americans might have interacted politically with one another, but their primary social and cultural relationships were with the land itself. In the words of one writer, the natural features of the landscape recognizable to Native Americans, such as the Rio Grande, were "timeless and impersonal." The river and the rest of the land "assume meaning," at least as some sort of boundary, "only in terms of the people who came to [settle on it]."[10] The frontier, in other words, became such only when people who conceived of it as the edge of empire, people with specific local and imperial agendas, took up residence.

Over time, the process of giving the land a political definition, first as a frontier and then as a border, unfolded. The physical place moved along a path marked by slow changes imperceptible to the people experiencing them at the time. Historians have a tendency to section events into periods, however, and so it is with their interpretations of the evolution of the U.S.-Mexico boundary. Patricia Nelson Limerick, for example, divided the story of the border into four phases, moving successively from imperial control, through periods of Mexican rule and then conflict with America, winding up finally in the modern phase of American domination.[11] David Lorey suggested three phases, with the final one divisible into parts identified by the predominant forms of economic activity. Lorey began with a frontier period of imperial administration, a Mexican era in which the borderlands begin to form, one subsequent period of primarily American economic dominance after the war of 1846 to 1848, and of American wealth predicated on Mexican labor.[12] Regardless of the exact chronology or the labels used, it appears that, by rough consensus, the border's past begins with Spanish imperial colonization and the frontier the Spanish chose to imagine.

Spain wasted little time in giving substance to the America they claimed to have discovered. The place that the United States and Mexico would someday fight over, the expanse of territory across which the two countries would trace out their boundary line, began to develop in the mid-1500s and quickly became a vibrant and dynamic region. Within this region, a local community emerged not long after the Spaniards found silver in its dry hills. The Spanish, working near Zacatecas in 1546, uncovered substantial deposits of silver. Four years later, a similar strike was made at Guanajuato. Mining operations began almost immediately, as did the formation of settlements designed to provide goods and services to the mine operators. Miners needed a variety of products—food, leather, cloth, iron, and wood—as well as services, such as weaving, blacksmithing, carpentry, and shoemaking. To meet the demand, suppliers and service providers organized their activities around large and small farms that functioned at the same time as agricultural and light-industrial centers. These *ranchos* represented far more than ranches in the modern sense. They served as critical additions that made mining not only profitable but also possible in the first place.[13]

Where one finds people and economic activity, one eventually finds social organization and, most important, culture. The cultural settlement of the Spanish frontier was facilitated by and rooted in the system of Catholic missions that anchored the imperial periphery during the colonial period. As focal points for religious devotion and social interaction, the missions lent cohesion and stability to the communities taking shape throughout the frontier region. The religious who supervised the mission system helped ensure order and, by paying for mission construction and operation themselves, allowed the royal government to defray (pay for) a substantial portion of the overall cost of colonization. Perhaps of greatest significance was the fact that missions acted as visible reminders of Spanish culture. The beliefs, practices, rituals, and ideas that Spanish officials hoped to transplant to the New World came neatly packaged in the subtle blend of ethnic pride and cultural superiority displayed by the missions. The missions brought Spain to the frontier and reconstructed it there for all to see.

After the ranchos and missions, the presidios represented the final element in the creation of a Spanish frontier community. These forts extended Spanish military power far beyond the limits of the viceregal rule around Mexico City and established an

THE CROWDED CONTINENT

Spain's empire in the New World was not alone. Two other very powerful colonial enterprises operated next door to the one Spain oversaw. To the east lay French territory, which until 1763 pushed up against the viceroyalty of New Spain along a line that ran from near New Orleans to the source of the Arkansas River. Beyond the French, hugging the Atlantic coastline, the English had planted colonies from just north of Florida to what is today Maine. Jockeying for advantage in trade, access to raw resources, and Indian relations, the three imperial powers acknowledged their borders officially but rarely respected them on a local level. French trappers and traders, in particular, routinely violated Spanish sovereignty. French missionaries also crossed into Spanish territory to compete with their Spanish counterparts for Indian souls. Both Catholic empires kept a watchful eye on the aggressively expansionist English colonies. Time and again, borders drawn boldly in Europe were ignored in North America. "With the French spreading all over the map," one writer remarked, "it was only a matter of time before they bumped into the English and the Spanish."* All three certainly did bump into one another's borders—and crossed them.

*Ted Morgan, *Wilderness at Dawn: The Settling of the North American Continent* (New York: Simon and Schuster, 1993), 206.

armed presence capable of keeping the local population in line, dealing with lingering Native American resistance to Spanish rule, and warding off encroachments by Spain's European competitors, England and France. The presidio system never fully lived up to expectations; it was chronically understaffed, poorly managed, and often ignored by the government. Still, the forts flew the royal standard (official flag), identifying the frontier and its inhabitants as Spanish possessions.

By 1600, this solid triad of rancho, mission, and presidio provided a scaffold for the building of a community with a singular frontier character and mindset that came to differ radically from those of the imperial authorities in the capital of New Spain. Population growth fed and animated the unnamed character of this frontier. As settlements spread, so did the inclination among settlers to identify locally rather than colonially. By 1574, 1,500 families had already moved from central Mexico to the banks of the Rio Grande.[14] Within 10 years, the entire lower portion of the Great River had been colonized. From there, the frontier crept westward. Santa Fe was established in 1610; Albuquerque began its history in 1706. Spanish settlers reached the California coast in the late eighteenth century, and they founded a mission and presidio along the shores of San Francisco Bay in 1776. A tiny village called Yerba Buena sprang up next, a cluster of shacks that would be transformed into the city of San Francisco during the Mexican-American War.

With economy, society, and culture firmly anchored from the Gulf of Mexico to the Pacific Ocean, the frontier advanced rapidly along a path increasingly divergent from that taken by the larger Spanish empire in America. The frontier was becoming a separate and different place. David Lorey concluded that this time was a transformative period in which "frontier life ... took on processes and structures all its own ... increasingly characterized by a unique and defining culture."[15]

Politics was one structure that took on the look of the frontier. The lax Spanish attitude toward colonial administration fostered a sense of independence in the northern settlements.

The viceregal bureaucrats in Mexico City governed the frontier with a remarkably light hand. This resulted in part from sheer distance: The frontier was far away from the center of power, and, in an age before timely reliable overland communication, distance mattered. Furthermore, the size of the region in question meant that many parts never received a great deal of notice from the colonial administration. For the most part, imperial officials remained content with this situation; few of them relished the prospect of leaving the material comforts of Mexico City for some dry, dusty, fly-ridden northern outpost. Unless Native American resistance flared up or some other European power showed a little too much interest, imperial authorities essentially ignored the frontier, leaving it to its own devices and course of development.

The Spanish version of benign neglect, a practice England and its colonies perfected and employed expertly, out of necessity produced a strong sense of regional autonomy and a habit of local affiliation along the frontier. The people of la frontera thus came to think of themselves as belonging to a distinct community situated in a coherent, contiguous physical reality. A similar, if somewhat less geographically specific, self-conception eventually manifested itself throughout Mexico. Dissatisfaction with imperial rule grew to the point of open defiance, which was followed by revolution. With its imperial power well past its prime and its royal treasury empty, Spain struggled to hold onto Mexico. Political exhaustion, however, compounded by a military coup in Madrid, convinced the Spanish king to relinquish control over the Mexicans; the viceroy grudgingly acknowledged their independence in 1821.

Over the course of nearly three centuries, a place had come into existence, carved out of the barren deserts and lush river bottoms of the frontier by potent social and cultural forces. As Spain withdrew from the New World, leaving an independent Mexican state behind, some things stayed the same and others changed radically. The center-periphery relationship between Mexico City and the frontier remained unaltered, with all of its

As soon as Mexico won its independence from Spain, Mexico had to deal with the aggressively expansionist United States. The United States had a foothold in Texas by the early nineteenth century and many American colonists rushed south to inhabit the region. In this mural, colonists gather near Bay City, Texas in 1821 as Stephen Austin issues land to them.

costs and benefits, agreements and disagreements. Three years after independence, however, the birth of the Mexican Republic as a constitutional entity confirmed the presence and significance of the far north by transforming it from an imperial frontier to a national boundary. The border area consequently acquired new value as a barrier against an already aggressively expansionist United States.

This buffering role, in the end, carried with it unintended consequences. Being so close to and yet so far from the United States, the border proved to be irresistibly attractive to an entirely new cast of players whose presence would complicate matters both within the border and between it and the Mexican government. These people, arriving first as barely tolerable but much-needed guest workers, then later as unwelcome, arguably illegal immigrants, accelerated the process of community formation, first along the Rio Grande and eventually all the way to California. These Americans, planting themselves most firmly in Texas and California, forced their way into the permanent order either by weaving themselves into Mexican society or by becoming Mexican citizens, albeit fractious (unruly) and combative ones. In this manner, the American immigrants of the early nineteenth century became part of the border mix rather than languishing on its fringes as mere opportunistic transients. This hard-won status as American Mexicans proved to be the catalyst that not only transformed the frontier into a genuine border, but also provoked the war that drove the United States and Mexico to the negotiating table at Guadalupe Hidalgo.

3

Transitions:
Tejanos to Texans,
Californios to
Californians,
1821–1846

Mexico's future seemed bright as the transformation from colonial outpost to independent republic began. Yet from the outset, problems arose. The new nation's political system would have to be constructed from the ground up. Without Spanish troops, Mexico had no army. Worst of all, the republic inherited a weak, backward economic structure from the Spanish colonial administration. Looking northward, the Mexicans imagined that they saw remedies to these and other problems in the future development of the frontier region. Texas farms, California cattle ranches, and Sonoran mines, it was believed, held out hope for profit and prosperity, providing wealth for the local economy while filling the national treasury with money to fund government programs. Furthermore, through northern development, Mexico could engage the United States peacefully as a valued neighbor. American expansionism, already a threat to Mexican sovereignty, could be effectively checked if Mexico was able to draw the Americans into a mutually beneficial trading and commercial relationship. In military terms, the buffering function of the frontier might be exploited by encouraging Mexican immigration and settlement of the area, thus ensuring Mexican security without an expensive deployment of soldiers, which the republic did not possess in fixed garrisons yet. The north promised much; the problem lay in the fact that vast stretches of it, even parts well suited to settlement and agriculture, sat vacant. Like Spain before it, Mexico would have to populate the frontier before taking advantage of it.

Traditionally, however, Mexicans proved reluctant to exchange the comforts of central Mexico for the rugged, hard life of the frontier. Few people found the harshness and isolation of the north appealing. Even if people had been willing to relocate in sufficient numbers, neither Mexicans as a whole nor their government had the requisite (needed) commercial, agricultural, and trading experience to realize the region's potential. Colonial trade under the Spanish had been limited and was dominated by the needs and interests of the parent country. As yet, there was no Mexican middle class, no business class accustomed to private investment in risky ventures, such as frontier development. Nor did the Mexicans have a heritage of uprooting themselves and heading to the edge of civilization in pursuit of a better life. Imperial colonization patterns generally had been determined and tightly controlled by the Spanish viceregal administration. Even if this had not been the case, Mexican society had never put a premium on the type of geographic mobility and transient mindset that was necessary to energize frontier settlement.

Mexico needed exactly the kind of qualities the Americans had been cultivating for more than 200 years. American expansionism had already pushed the frontiers of that country to the edge of Mexican territory and seemed ready to spill American settlers into the new republic whether the government in Mexico City liked it or not. This relentless movement could be resisted, but the more advantageous course would be to tap into the American expansionist impulse and harness it to serve Mexican ends. Offer the Americans exactly what they sought so desperately in the early nineteenth century—land, in this instance, Mexican land. Rather than trying to blunt the westward momentum of American growth, the Mexican government decided to channel it and to manipulate it for the young nation's own good. Let American farmers till the Texas soil; let American entrepreneurs invest the needed capital to build an export market in California. If this meant sharing the frontier culturally, accepting alien influences, and tolerating foreign ways, then so be it. The anticipated final result, a secure and prosperous Mexico, justified such accommodations.

When the time came, the Mexican government did not have to look very far for American candidates willing to live in this proposed shared space along the old frontier. The Spanish colonial government, on the eve of granting Mexican independence in 1821, had already given permission for a group of Americans to settle north of the Rio Grande in the area they called Tejas, which the Americans would quickly christen Texas. Led by

Moses Austin, the company comprised 300 families from Missouri. Ignorant of the disturbances in Spain, specifically a military coup that threatened to bring down the monarchy, Austin's band did not notice their patrons' distraction. As a result, they had begun their journey south before news of Mexico's newly won independent status reached them. The immigrants, having renounced their American citizenship, were technically subjects of the Spanish crown and had no political affiliation with Mexico as a separate entity. Mexican authorities, desiring the American migration to continue, smoothed out this wrinkle by automatically granting the immigrants Mexican citizenship and welcoming them as Mexicans.

Just as the government had hoped, the newcomers brought with them a powerful work ethic, strong backs, and a solid background in farming virgin soil. Their wagons, however, also carried a cargo of aggressive individualism, a preference for local autonomy, and an abiding suspicion of central power. These traits made some in Mexico uneasy. The frontier needed people, and everyone recognized that; however, the republicans in Mexico City just as urgently needed to consolidate control and to establish clear lines of authority emanating from the capital. The Americans might turn out to be impediments or, worse, might balk stubbornly when the government in Mexico City asserted itself. The immigrants could wind up being more trouble than they were worth. Still, the Americans had come and they intended to stay.

For the time being, tolerance, however grudging, guided relations between the frontier and the Mexican government. Stephen Austin, who succeeded Moses, his father, after the latter's death, actively sought American integration into Mexican society, culture, and politics. He understood that the process of American colonization could be reversed at any time if the immigrants caused trouble. He could not afford to make the government regret the American presence in Texas; he had to cultivate an image of the colonists as loyal Mexican citizens. Austin, in fact, wanted American rights codified. To this end,

STEPHEN F. AUSTIN.

After Mexico gained independence from Spain in 1821, the country welcomed the American immigrants who inhabited the region of Texas and pushed down into Mexico City. Led by Stephen Austin, shown in this portrait, the colonists fulfilled Mexico's desperate need for hard workers and knowledgeable farmers on the frontier.

Austin assured the central government that he, and, by extension, his people, stood "determined to fulfill rigidly all the duties and obligations of a Mexican citizen."[16] In return, Austin petitioned the government to guarantee American freedoms in writing. He requested that American immigrant rights be spelled out on paper as clearly as those of native Mexicans. After some discussion, officials in Mexico City acceded to Austin's demands. In 1824, while drafting a constitution for all Mexicans, the central government passed a law specifically confirming the liberties of Texans within the republic. Supplemental legislation, tacked on a year later, recognized Austin as the spokesperson for the American settlers on the Rio Grande.

A signal victory had been won, all the more so because it came in the midst of remarkable changes in the composition of the frontier population. From 1821 to 1836, the number of Americans living along the Great River multiplied. A 30 percent increase in the number of Mexican Tejanos notwithstanding, Anglo Texans became a majority by 1830. This led to a corresponding increase in American influence, but, more important, a new local identity began to reveal itself. No longer all one or all the other, Anglo Texans came to conceive of themselves as American Mexicans, living in a place distinct from both the America they had left and the Mexico they had entered. As early as 1832, Austin was making regular trips to Mexico City to argue for recognition of specifically northern interests, shared by Anglos and Mexicans alike. His entreaties eventually became a call for Texas statehood within the federal republic. "Texas needs a government, and the best she can have," Austin pleaded, "is to be created a State in the Mexican Federation.... The character of the people of Texas," he contended, was already and would remain "*Mexico-Texan.*"[17] By this time, Austin himself had been so utterly absorbed by the frontier that he took to ending his personal correspondence with a hearty "Adios."[18]

The creation of a border community was well under way in Texas before the first Americans began slowly drifting into California. As the northwestern extreme of Mexico, California experienced a process of community formation decidedly different from that found along the banks of the Rio Grande. The eventual outcome was the same, however: Californians, like Texans, crafted their own local patterns of cooperation and conflict with little reference to the national agendas of either Mexico or the United States. Those national agendas would infringe on and often disrupt, but never prescribe, local development.

While under Spanish rule, California followed a standard colonial model of settlement and organization. Pressing northward in the late eighteenth century, Spain founded a chain of missions and presidios from San Diego to the bay of San Francisco along a broken, rutted road going by the grandiose title of the King's Highway, El Camino Real. These establishments were followed promptly by ranchos set up to exploit the potential for lucrative cattle ranching on the flat grasslands of the San Joaquin Valley. The traditional tripartite arrangement of missions, presidios, and ranchos that dominated California's early history represented a familiar axis of sociocultural, political, and economic institutions. Of course, overseas trade via San Francisco, the finest natural harbor on the Pacific Coast, offered a novel opportunity for profit, if properly managed. Asia, China in particular, represented a vast marketplace that had only begun to be penetrated by European powers such as Spain. California's prospects loomed large, but Spain ran out of time. Mexico inherited California along with the rest of the frontier, and now it stood to gain from this most distant territory.

One obstacle loomed, however: California, like Texas, suffered from a chronic and debilitating shortage of one resource— people. The land lacked farmers to work its soil, ranchers to raise its herds of cattle, and entrepreneurs to market its produce. Ranchos could produce food, as well as a host of other commodities. Traders, operating along the coast, especially out of San Francisco Bay, could then ship those products across the Pacific to Asia or around the tip of South America to markets in the eastern United States. The sale of California grain, beef, tallow, and leather could bring in vast sums of money, but it all depended on people. Mexico needed to populate California. Among Mexicans at the time, however, "to speak of California was like mentioning the end of the world."[19] Some adventurous or perceptive men and women recognized the potential of California and moved north, but most Mexicans wanted nothing to do with it. By the late 1820s, the Mexican government had become so desperate for settlers that it began releasing prisoners on parole and transporting them to California. Two hundred such criminals were sent north as "settlers" in 1829 alone; 130 followed the next year.[20] These men, called *cholos*, roughly translated as "scoundrels," contributed nothing more than drunkenness, brawling, and an occasional murder to the local scene. An ill-conceived program from its inception, letting felons loose in California convinced Californios, as those who moved north referred to themselves, that the central government ignored the territory's interests and did not understand its problems. As in Texas, a worldview had begun to form in which the local community viewed itself paradoxically as part of, yet distinct from, the larger Mexican republic. According to the historian Leonard Pitt, a movement that contrasted local norms to "the 'degraded' influences of Mexico," started and "made men conscious of their California birth. In response to the new identity, [people] ceased calling themselves *Españoles* or *Mexicanos* and began to insist on the name *Californios*."[21]

As the Californio identity took shape, the local community received its first significant infusion of non-Mexican newcomers. During the 1830s, Americans began migrating to the Pacific Coast. Although Russians and Englishmen had dabbled in settling California and flirted with the idea of immigration, their impact would be minimal; Americans stood as the real prize. Americans, in raw numbers, would bring much-needed skills and capital. Their ways and beliefs would certainly be different, but the Californios welcomed diversity and saw strength in a local blend of American and Mexican traditions. Simply filling up the territory's open spaces seemed to be a worthy goal. If Americans could also wring more from the land and develop an export market, so much the better.

The first good chance to see the fruits of American immigration came in 1834. Under the leadership of Antonio López de Santa Anna, the Mexican government embarked on a program of radical secularization. Santa Anna, and many other Mexicans, felt that the power of the Roman Catholic Church impeded Mexican social progress and acted as a drag on economic modernization. The Church's influence, therefore, had to be neutralized. In California this translated into the dismantling of the mission system and the redistribution of thousands of acres of land to the ranchos. Suddenly, California became attractive to land-hungry Americans. Between 1834 and 1846, 700 separate land grants were awarded in California, most to Americans.[22] During that same period, American merchants and traders discovered in San Francisco Bay's placid waters and snug coves a possible area of intermediate shipping trade that could turn California into one of the world's great marketplaces. As increasing numbers of Americans intermingled with established Californios, a local culture that both reflected and rejected those of Mexico and the United States began to emerge. A community started to grow up around a local set of assumptions and values, a people and an order apart.

Californios and American immigrants alike benefited from Mexico's policy changes of the 1830s. Criticism of the central government, therefore, remained serious but muted. The people found Mexican rule distasteful but not intolerable. Timely agitation among influential landholders and the commercial elite compelled the Mexican governors of the territory to rule with a degree of circumspection (caution) and restraint. No territorial executive wanted to openly challenge the emerging capitalist class. As it was, the chief administrators of California found themselves in the awkward position of overseeing an emerging local community prepared to detach itself from the rest of the republic. Antagonizing the landed gentry would do nothing but cause trouble. Californios were content with the advantages of secularization and demanded only the right to speak their minds and demonstrate their local allegiance. No matter how much the Mexican governors might have wanted it to be otherwise, California was drifting out of Mexico's orbit. Their favored response was not to accelerate the movement by acting

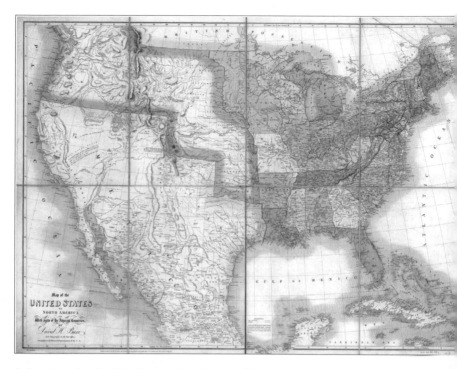

Before the outbreak of the Mexican-American war, Mexico possessed most of the lands that today make up Texas, California, and the Southwest United States, as seen in this 1839 map.

precipitously and antagonizing the local community. This moderation stopped California from breaking into open rebellion, as Texas soon did.

In Texas, similar developments led the periphery to peel itself away from the center in a quest for political independence. Santa Anna's push to centralize power in Mexico City by dismembering the mission system expanded opportunities in California but choked them off in Texas. The legislative initiatives of the 1830s had an entirely different impact in Texas, resulting in the lessening of traditional liberties and the limiting of local opportunities. Texans and Tejanos watched their world shrink as the central government asserted its authority along the Rio Grande to a far greater extent than it ever did in California. By 1835, government intrusion in Texas had become almost intolerable. The government in Mexico City exerted more pressure on Texas than it did on California, most likely because of the Rio Grande's much smaller population (relative to that of California), the heavy American influence along the Rio Grande, and the area's strategic position in relation to the United States. After a series of minor local uprisings against the central government on both sides of the Great River, Santa Anna's regime tightened restrictions on further immigration, eventually barring it altogether; pressured Anglo Texans to end slavery and then did it for them; and denied repeated requests for additional law courts. The last

SETTLING IN

Despite many similarities, Texas and California represented two quite different models of American integration into the preexisting Mexican social order. Steven Austin's colony along the Rio Grande reveled in its independence and resembled more of an ethnic enclave than an integral part of the established society. Although Austin and his fellow Anglo Texans could not help but be influenced profoundly by their Mexican neighbors, neither he nor his compatriots immersed themselves into the local culture to the extent that Americans in California did. California Yankees regularly and unabashedly married into prominent Mexican families, absorbing their traditions and beliefs; held Mexican land grants; and even participated in local politics with gusto. Many Californians, in fact, gained relatively high office and prestige and took their positions as Mexican officials seriously. Estaban Richardson, son of San Francisco's first American resident, William Richardson, and his Mexican wife, looked back in 1918 and remembered how proud his father had been of his appointment as port captain by then-governor José Figueroa. "My father," wrote the younger Richardson, "was appointed the harbor caption of the port at Yerba Buena, later designated San Francisco. For acting in this capacity, the Mexican government, always short of cash, but liberal in land, granted my father a vast concession."* The land given to the Richardson family stretched into Mendocino County far to the north of San Francisco and established William Richardson as a member of the California elite. Unfortunately, the United States government later refused to recognize the Richardson title, and seized the land in question.

* Malcolm E. Barker, *San Francisco Memoirs, 1835–1851: Eyewitness Accounts of the Birth of a City*. San Francisco: Londonborn Publications, 1994, p. 66.

straw came when the national government refused to consider Texans' demand that it be separated from the state of Coahuila, to which it had been attached by the constitution of 1824. The central authorities also began to monitor the activities of Texans who argued for broader autonomy, and, in what was viewed as a direct threat to liberty, the Mexican government dispatched troops to the Rio Grande in an attempt to dissuade anyone, Texan or Tejano, who contemplated independence.

The Mexican government had no intention of allowing a group of foreign immigrants to run roughshod over the power of the central authorities, especially when those settlers exhibited a fiercely local sense of independence. Slavery only compounded the problem. In the early nineteenth century, Mexico followed the global trend toward abolition; the American immigrants, in their support of slavery, thus represented a throwback to an earlier tradition. Anglo Texans held to racial and ethnic concepts that were inconsistent with the demands of modernization in their own country, let alone those in a relatively new nation such as Mexico, determined to rapidly build an independent economy and political order. Mexican politicians, no doubt, also saw the bitterness and division the issue of slavery had begun to cause for the Americans and wanted none of it. Polarization along the lines of what was taking place in the United States was the last thing Mexico needed. Texas would have to be brought to heel.

Stephen Austin, exhausted and fearing the worst, pleaded with those in the national capital to recognize Texas's peculiar circumstances and its special position within the federal republic. Santa Anna, however, ignored Austin's supplications. In a fit of passion, the normally reserved and thoughtful Austin wrote in a letter that, "If the people of Texas do not take affairs into their own hands, that land is lost." He concluded by proclaiming the Texas cause a righteous one; he signed his correspondence, "Dios y Texas," God and Texas.[23] Once he collected himself, Austin returned to lobbying for peaceful reform. His compatriots back home had other ideas: Anglo Texans began to take up arms. Volunteer militia companies formed all along the Rio Grande; this was a serious turn of events that the Mexican government could not and did not ignore.

The central government moved decisively to end Texas's autonomous aspirations. Santa Anna, determined to "punish that band of ungrateful foreigners," announced his intention "that the most active measures be taken, measures required by the very nature of what is in reality a crime against the whole nation."[24] To carry this out, in December 1835, Santa Anna ordered General Martin Cos to move up the Rio Grande and suppress the insurrectionist (rebellious) spirit of the Texans. Cos's appearance in a region unaccustomed to seeing Mexican soldiers and resentful of their presence provoked the Texans into open revolt. For the next seven months, the center and periphery, Mexico and Texas, battled one another in a brief but bloody war.

By February 1836, Santa Anna had entered the fray, leading an army into San Antonio. He found the town itself undefended but noticed that the local mission, known as the Alamo, had been fortified by the rebels. As he took up positions around it, Santa Anna saw that the Texans had hoisted a flag over the structure that combined the Mexican national colors—red, white, and green—with two stars, one for Texas and another for its companion state, Coahuila. Even in resistance to Mexican rule, the Texans proclaimed their shared heritage with the Mexican state to which they were officially joined. For weeks, Santa Anna laid siege to the Alamo before capturing the mission in a final assault that took the lives of 187 Texans who fought to the death rather than surrender. The death toll nearly doubled some days later when the Mexicans captured and executed 300 Americans at Goliad. The Mexicans termed it an execution of traitors; the Texans remembered it as a massacre of innocent hostages. Finally, in April 1836, Santa Anna, once more in personal command of a large Mexican force, accepted defeat at the battle of San Jacinto. Bested by a Texan army led by Sam Houston, Santa Anna acceded to Texas's demand for independence. The Treaty of Velasco (May 1836) ended not only the war but also a relationship between Mexico and Texas that had lasted for almost three centuries. One part of the Mexican frontier had detached itself violently and permanently from the rest of the republic.

The central authorities worried briefly that California might follow Texas's lead and prepared for any eventuality along the Pacific Coast. The community there, however, had no inclination toward armed insurrection. Californios had always kept a lower profile, so they attracted little federal attention. Their resentment of Mexican rule was thus proportionately reduced. Americans in California had blended more smoothly into local society and culture, making their presence less intensely felt and less of an irritant than in Texas. California was also farther from the center of national authority than Texas and so more easily escaped notice. Mexican governors did not impose themselves on the territory, and the local community was content to bide its time and wait for Mexican power to wane of its own accord. A great California war of independence was not destined to take place.

By 1836, the frontier had begun the torturous process of becoming a borderland. The Treaty of Velasco had only roughly sketched the contours of the newly independent Texas, and much, including the precise location of Texas's border with Mexico, remained in dispute. Tentative lines were being drawn, however, lines that represented an artificial division of the local American-Mexican community and that split that community into two presumably antagonistic halves. No one knew what impact these arbitrary borders would have locally, but the structure of border society was already too complex and its culture too nuanced to be so effortlessly divided. The tendency toward a cohesive border community was irreversible.

By the time the United States and Mexico moved closer to war over border issues, a scaffolding had been put in place within which new realities and identities would be constructed across the old frontier. The new border community would become part of, yet would remain separate from, the larger nations to its north and south. What began to emerge from the Rio Grande to California was a developmentally unique and internally driven local order. Conflict and cooperation would coexist within this order, but not in isolation. The Mexican and American national governments took a renewed interest in the old frontier by the mid-1840s. A bitter conflict loomed, conflict that found expression in war and settlement in the Treaty of Guadalupe Hidalgo.

4

Mexico, America, and the Border at War, 1846–1847

The geographic place of which Texas and California were parts now advanced to a new stage in its evolution. Beginning as a thinly settled imperial frontier, it became a bicultural transitional zone where different elements were slowly combining to form the seed of a vibrant, if quarrelsome, regional community. Despite all its power to reshape attitudes, assumptions, and worldviews locally, though, the border area functioned nationally as a boundary between two maturing republics, so outside pressures could and did act on it. These forces came from the north and the south simultaneously, alternately pressing in on the border and pulling it apart. They emanated from political leaders in Washington and Mexico City, who showed neither concern for nor interest in matters such as cultural blending or gradual transitions between Mexican and American realities. The governments had other agendas. The border region, just entering the first stages in the formative process of local development, tried to resist outside influences and sought to define itself in terms that proved locally beneficial and sensible. California and Texas needed time; they were just beginning to create themselves. The national governments of the United States and Mexico were not inclined to wait.

In California, both native Mexicans and American transplants toyed with the idea of independence from Mexico on and off throughout the late 1830s and early 1840s. Their grumbling, however, came to nothing. The occasional urge to separate California from the republic sprang out of momentary fits of resentment. Incompetent governors, boorish soldiers swaggering around beyond the presidio gates, and feelings of estrangement from the social swirl of Mexico proper made independence seem attractive now and then, but no single complaint ever resonated deeply enough to lead to rebellion—at least not yet.

Californians mused over and murmured about rebellion, but Texas had actually rebelled. From 1836 to 1845, Texas was an independent state, albeit one sandwiched uncomfortably between a Mexico that never accepted Texas's separation as legal or permanent and an American nation enthusiastically embracing a concept known as Manifest Destiny. Part of an ideology of "divinely" inspired and sanctioned geopolitical expansion, Manifest Destiny became central to American culture in the 1840s. First pronounced in 1845 by newspaper editor John O'Sullivan in the pages of the *Democratic Review*, Manifest Destiny proclaimed that America's "destiny was to overspread the whole North American continent with an immense democratic population."[25] America had a God-given right to expand, even if it was done at the expense of the country's neighbors.

Manifest Destiny and the thinking on which it was based operated as a direct challenge to Mexico. Everyone understood that American expansion could take place only in the West and Southwest, Mexico's traditional domain. Conflict had to occur, and it would most likely take place along the Rio Grande. Here, both the Mexican desire to protect its territorial integrity and the American obsession with continental domination clashed most openly—with Texas in the middle. On the one hand, Texas had to fend off Mexican efforts to reclaim the former province; on the other hand, it needed to seek the support and protection of the United States without being utterly subordinated to yet another distant, detached national government. Texas rightfully viewed both Washington, D.C., and Mexico City with suspicion. Neither capital, it was believed, comprehended the reality of life along the border or cared very much about such a distant place. Still, Texas could not stay outside the orbits of both national centers forever; either the relationship with Mexico would be patched up or closer ties with the United States would be cultivated. As it turned out, fate and a determined American president, John Tyler, settled the matter in the spring of 1845.

Tyler had been a champion of Texas annexation throughout his presidency, brief though it was. Tyler came on the scene in 1841, when the untimely death of William Henry Harrison propelled him into the White House. From that point on, Tyler urged Congress to invite Texas into the Union. His exertions had nothing to do with the interests of Texans. Tyler hoped that annexing Texas would be the first step not only in grabbing the rest of the continent for the United States but also in guaranteeing the future of Southern slavery. Getting ahold of territory along the Rio Grande would satisfy expansionists, who envisioned an American nation stretching from coast to coast, and would please Southern slaveholders who sought more soil for their involuntary servants to till.

Tyler neither understood nor cared to understand the border on its own terms. In fact, the president timed his push for annexation according to his own political fortunes. After he left the Democratic Party and his support of slavery earned him the enmity of his current colleagues in the Whig Party, Tyler knew he would never be elected in his own right. He had nothing to lose in pushing the Texas issue in Congress. In March 1845, with only one day left in office, Tyler succeeded in convincing Congress to annex Texas. The offer was made, and Texas accepted in July. Mexico responded by severing diplomatic relations with the United States and putting itself on a war footing.[26] In one fell swoop, Texas's quarrel with Mexico became an international dispute. The border periphery now had two centers to deal with.

The source of all the trouble lay in the fact that Texas and Mexico had never officially agreed on a border that put the former partner states of Coahuila, Nuevo León, and Tamaulipas on one side and Texas on the other. During the Mexican period, Texas and Coahuila had been considered one state, with an informal division at the Nueces River. Most Texans and Mexicans presumed that this would remain the case after independence in 1836. The Treaty of Velasco, however, stipulated that Mexican troops had to withdraw from Texas territory beyond the Rio Grande. Thus, many national political leaders in the United States, unfamiliar with the history of Mexican Texas, claimed that the Rio Grande represented the true border.

Both national governments had ulterior motives in this argument. Mexico sought a Nueces boundary so that it could gain access to the rich, fertile bottomlands north of the Rio Grande

James K. Polk, United States president from 1845 until 1849, was elected on a platform of expansion and the idea of Manifest Destiny. Polk succeeded in acquiring the Oregon Territory and pressured Mexico to cede Texas, New Mexico, and California, which led to war in 1846.

River. This area offered agricultural opportunities that did not exist in most parts of the Mexican north. Moreover, the land had already been brought under the plow by industrious Texans; it would cost the Mexican government very little to reap substantial rewards. The United States insisted on the Rio Grande in order to profit from the gulf port at the mouth of the river. American farmers in Texas needed the Rio Grande as a highway down which they could easily and inexpensively ship their produce into the Gulf of Mexico and to points beyond. Farms sprawled along the banks of the Rio Grande; river traffic was their lifeblood. A Nueces border simply would not do. The United States had to have the Great River. The location of the international boundary thus became the primary irritant in United States–Mexico relations and a reason for war in 1846.

Texas magnified national tensions, but American ambitions and the Mexican determination to thwart them reached far beyond the muddy Rio Grande—they reached all the way to the western horizon, in fact. The United States eyed California greedily. Although the border in Texas was an immediate concern, drawing a similar line that made California an American territory became an equally important objective. California was the prize in the Far West. No one could fault the United States for coveting California's rich, fertile valleys perfect for farming; lush grasslands ready to be grazed by herds of cattle; waters teeming with fish, whales, and otters; and, of course, the harbor of San Francisco, gateway to the Pacific and key to the China trade. Mexico, a young and proud nation, desired to hold onto California for the very same reasons, as well as for national honor and territorial sovereignty. Both nations had their agendas; neither felt much inclined toward compromise. War suddenly became a realistic option for both governments. The border community would suffer for it.

International tension grew during the winter and spring of 1846. Determined to free itself for possible action against Mexico, the United States finally settled its longstanding dispute with Great Britain over the other border, the one with British Canada. In June 1846, the United States and Great Britain signed the Oregon Treaty, giving America control over the area of the Pacific Northwest that would eventually become the states of Oregon and Washington. With this matter taken care of, the focus returned to the Rio Grande.

The United States government might have been eager for a fight, but a sizable pro-war faction existed in Mexico as well. These politicians and generals embraced war as a cure for Mexico's political and economic ills, and they genuinely anticipated victory. Mexico's army was fairly well equipped and four times the size of its adversary's. Foreign observers agreed that the Mexican forces were more than capable of answering any American challenge. The London *Times*, in fact, contended flatly that the republic's armies "are superior to those of the United States."[27] Confident in its military, Mexico prepared for war. The United States, equally sure of victory and even more impatient to see hostilities begin, did likewise. Last-minute negotiations, doomed from the start because of a mutual refusal to compromise, failed miserably.

Claiming that Mexico had sabotaged any chance for peace, the American president in 1846, James K. Polk, ordered troops under the command of General Zachary Taylor to advance from their station in Louisiana and take up positions along the Rio Grande, south of the Nueces River, in the area claimed by Mexico. Although Polk, an ardent supporter of the Manifest Destiny doctrine, christened Taylor's force the Army of Observation, its true purpose was apparent: to provoke Mexico and turn the border into a war zone. Taylor's troops appeared across the river from the Mexican city of Matamoros in March 1846. On April 23, the Mexican congress voted for a declaration of war.

For the next three weeks, fighting raged along the Rio Grande. The opposing armies fought bloody battles in Texas at Palo Alto (May 8) and Resaca de la Palma (May 9), in which American technology and tactics overcame raw Mexican courage to produce important American victories. Finally, on May 13, the U.S. Congress legitimated the fighting by declaring war on Mexico. Freed from all political technicalities, Taylor's army splashed across the Rio Grande and struck the Mexicans in Nuevo León at Monterrey. Defeating the Mexicans easily there, Taylor moved south and occupied the town of Saltillo, halting his progress to await the outcome of operations already under way in central Mexico aimed at taking Mexico City itself.

Far to the south of Taylor, General Winfield Scott launched a daring amphibious assault against Vera Cruz in January 1847. After a ferocious bombardment, Scott took the city and advanced inland toward the Mexican capital. Meanwhile,

The United States annexed Texas in 1845, and by early 1846 the United States was at war with Mexico over the border between the two countries. In one of the earliest battles, at Palo Alto, Texas on May 8, advanced military technology and tactics helped the American forces overcome Mexico in an important victory.

General Santa Anna, hoping to buy time and disrupt American plans, struck northward against Taylor. The opposing armies met in February 1847 at Buena Vista and fought a two-day battle that ended in a draw. The diversion of scarce men and supplies from the main theater of operations in central Mexico, however, cost Santa Anna dearly. Unable to drive the Americans out of the northern reaches of the republic and facing a relentless American advance in the south, Santa Anna asked Scott for an armistice in August and began preparing for full-scale peace negotiations. Poisoned by suspicion and crippled by disagreements within and between both parties, the talks went nowhere. Frustrated and angry, Scott renewed his push toward Mexico City and captured the capital on September 14. With that, the war throughout Mexico, and along the Rio Grande, came to a halt.

The fighting in the border region of Texas scarred the local community badly. Farming had been disrupted, and order had broken down. The movement of armies through the land forced many people to leave their homes. Entire hamlets and villages emptied; large towns were occupied and put under military rule. Terror and atrocity multiplied. Ulysses S. Grant, of future Civil War fame, wrote that in the border city of Matamoros, "a great many murders have been committed." George Meade, another officer who played a major role in the Civil War, remarked how American soldiers "killed five or six innocent people walking in the street, for no other object than their own amusement." Adding to the border community's woes, Meade noted that the same soldiers also "rob and steal the cattle and corn of the poor farmers." Winfield Scott himself acknowledged that robbery, rape, and murder "have been common all along the Rio Grande." A Mexican newspaper summed up the impact of the American presence by labeling the soldiers "a horde of banditti ... thirsty with the desire to appropriate our riches... ."[28] In many instances, border people turned on their own, with some of the worst outrages against Mexican civilians committed by their American neighbors. Taylor himself noted that many of the Texans among his men perpetrated "some shameful atrocities."[29] Grant blamed most of the trouble in Matamoros on Texans who "seem to think it perfectly right to impose on the people of a conquered city to any extent, and even to murder them where the act can be covered by dark."[30]

Throughout the border region, not just along the Rio Grande, fear and anxiety cast long shadows. Over time, these emotions gave way to resentment and frustration. In some areas of American occupation, the border citizenry rose up against the "outsiders." Open rebellions broke out in Taos, New Mexico, and in Los Angeles, California. In Taos, where the uprising included "many of the most influential persons in the northern part of this territory," 150 people died in fierce fighting.[31] Los Angeles experienced an even larger revolt after the American commander there, Archibald Gillespie, took it upon himself to go about "humiliating the most respectable men."[32] This humiliation took its most extreme form in Gillespie's ill-advised attempt to confiscate privately held firearms. Resistance to his order was immediate, pronounced, and, in the end, effective.

It is true that the brunt of the wartime burden fell on Texas, but California suffered a no less wrenching experience. Los Angeles, as mentioned above, openly and violently defied American power. The town also hosted the only major battle of the war to take place outside of the Texas theater of operations: the battle of Los Angeles, in which Californio cavalry fought the technologically superior Americans to a draw. In Northern California, the conflict manifested itself in an attempt by

VOICES AGAINST THE WAR

The Mexican-American War, though in harmony with popular American thinking at the time regarding continental expansion, was far from universally supported. From all quarters came criticism of the war's aims and conduct. The American Anti-Slavery Society claimed that President Polk started the war "solely for the detestable and horrible purpose of extending and perpetuating American slavery throughout the territory of Mexico."* The abolitionist newspaper *The Liberator* labeled the conflict a war "of aggression, of invasion, of conquest, and rapine marked by ruffianism, perfidy, and every other feature of national depravity."** The newspaper's editor, the fiery abolitionist William Lloyd Garrison, went so far as to wish "the most utter defeat and disgrace" on the U.S. force fighting in Mexico. Horace Greeley of the *New York Tribune* wondered in its pages what the United States had to gain from all the death and destruction: "Who believes that a score of victories over Mexico, the 'annexation' of half her provinces, will give us more Liberty, a purer Morality, a more prosperous Industry, than we have now?"*** Such dissenting voices, however, were quickly stilled by a series of dramatic triumphs on the battlefield. At the time of the signing of the Treaty of Guadalupe Hidalgo, most of the American public agreed with the newspaper the *Whig Intelligencer*, which remarked that the nation's cause had been just and that the payment of $15 million to Mexico proved that "we take nothing by conquest ... Thank God."+

* Zinn, *People's History of the United States*, p. 155.

** Ibid., p. 157.

*** Ibid., p. 159.

+ Ibid., p. 169.

recently arrived American immigrants to "play the Texas game"[33] and establish a California republic. The Bear Flag Revolt, as it came to be called (after the somewhat comical flag thrown together by the "rebels," which was so badly designed that observers thought they saw a pig on it rather than the intended grizzly bear), degenerated into a farce. Many of the newcomers used the short-lived experiment in self-rule as an excuse to loot, abuse, and, in a few instances, murder Californios.[34] Only the arrival of American forces in July 1846 and the subsequent demise of the Bear Flag Republic brought some semblance of order and a return of limited authority to the Californios and the long-established Americans associated with them.

Major combat operations ended in 1847. Mexico had been defeated and its capital city occupied in September of that year. The republic's proud government had been humbled, its people uncertain as to what the future held. This uncertainty was felt more sharply along the border than anywhere else. From Texas to California, life had been disrupted at best; at worst, local institutions and relationships had been disassembled, pending reassembly through an American-dictated peace treaty. On both sides of the border, reality was about to be drastically altered. The process of drawing a boundary where none had existed before would soon start. The old order, which Mexicans and Americans had embraced, albeit with varying degrees of ambivalence, was slipping into history. The future had a line through it that carried far more positive connotations for the central governments that drew it than it did for the local community that had to live with it.

As the representatives of the United States and Mexico sat down at the negotiating table, they spread out a map and set to work determining where one nation, people, and culture ended and where the other began. In the end, the resulting international boundary, detailed in the peace treaty that would be signed just north of Mexico City, at the town of Guadalupe Hidalgo, came into focus more sharply for the outsiders who created it than it ever did for the border people who had to adjust to its presence. The crafting of a bicultural identity would proceed, but the resulting community would now be composed of a unique population with a distinct border ideality, as the Mexicans put it, *borderistas*.

5

Making
a Modern Border:
The Treaty of
Guadalupe Hidalgo

Representatives of the United States and Mexico met in January 1848 to establish, in the words of the treaty they would draft, "peace and friendship ... concord, harmony, and mutual confidence."[35] Along the way, they settled an array of issues concerning Mexican rights within the newly ceded territories, Native American relations, and commerce. The centerpiece of the proposed treaty, however, and the focal point for debates north and south of the proposed border, was the precise location of the international boundary.

The integrity and indeed the very placement of the border had been the immediate cause of the war and figured prominently in the secret discussions between the combatants that took place even as the fighting raged. Now, as the United States and Mexico faced one another across the negotiating table, the border stood out on the agenda. Nicholas P. Trist, an experienced diplomat and Southerner who spoke fluent Spanish, opened the talks with the paramount American demand. Trist insisted that Mexico recognize the Rio Grande as the eastern end of the border with an as-yet-undetermined extension to the Pacific coast south of San Diego. Trist's inclusion of San Diego in the deal reflected the belief at the time that the port would soon rival San Francisco in its value. Neither side knew at the moment just how much more important San Francisco would turn out to be: As the negotiations began, gold was discovered in the Sierra foothills just east of Sacramento. The Mexican delegation to the talks was open to Trist's demands. The men were prepared to concede the Rio Grande boundary and agree to an extension of the border that put San Diego in the American zone.

The delegates to the peace conference claimed to represent the interests of their respective nations. It is doubtful, though, that the needs of the border community figured highly in their plans. Despite the assertions in the first article of the draft treaty that the shared goal remained a "firm and universal peace between the United States and the Mexican Republic, and their ... territories ... without exception of places or persons,"[36] the representatives served as agents of the two central governments. The concerns of those governments took precedence over those of the border community, and chief among these concerns was the division of the disputed region, regardless of the local impact.

Article V of the treaty laid out the boundary line as clearly as possible along the Rio Grande–Gila–Colorado rivers axis. It dictated that "the Boundary line between the two Republics shall commence in the Gulf of Mexico ... opposite the mouth of the Rio Grande ... thence westwardly ... until it intersects the first branch of the river Gila."[37] This was the easy part. From the Colorado to the Pacific, the border would have to be surveyed. Even though the treaty stated that the boundary would simply follow "the division line between Upper and Lower California,"[38] the Mexicans were not sure exactly where that line lay. A simple remedy was proposed: Each government would appoint a border commissioner and surveyor to find it. Together, these men would "meet at the Port of San Diego, and proceed to run and mark the said Boundary."[39] With the procedure for finding and identifying the border set, the two countries were directed to respect each other's sovereignty by agreeing that the "Boundary line ... shall be religiously respected by each of the two Republics."[40] The two delegations felt satisfied with the border as they had drawn it. Secure separation of the two countries had been their goal, and they had achieved it. The utter artificiality of such a line in the context of the border community and its culture and society was not a consideration. The centers had spoken; the periphery would have to adjust and cope.

After agreeing on the fiction of a border, the negotiators turned to restructuring life along it. Article VI of the treaty dealt with the issue of river traffic. The border region's rivers always had been a shared resource, held and exploited in common by the local community. Now, national representatives took up the task of labeling the waters as being the property of either the United States or Mexico. The central governments set about deciding what could and could not be done, and by whom, along the Colorado, Gila, and Rio Grande rivers. Any railroad or canal project would necessarily "serve equally for the use and advantage of both countries," but the money for such projects, and thus control of them, obviously would come from investment sources outside of the local community.[41] Distant investors, often aligned with the national governments, had an interest in reducing local autonomy. The region that once received too little attention, and money, would now have too much, with mixed consequences.

The treaty next considered the people newly separated by the border. Because of the way the boundary had been drawn and the prevailing patterns of settlement, most Americans along the line wound up in the United States, but so did many Mexicans. Being trapped on the wrong side of this imaginary line, Mexicans suddenly became foreigners. Many uprooted themselves and their families and repatriated to the Mexican side, a movement actively encouraged by the Mexican government as a way to quickly populate its side of the border. Many other border Mexicans remained, seeing no real advantage in leaving one part of their home for another simply to have a different national flag flying over their heads. With the stroke of a pen, these people, became Mexican Americans, and it was for them that Article VIII of the Treaty of Guadalupe Hidalgo was written.

Of all the treaty articles, this one stood out as the most likely candidate for flagrant violation. Theoretically, Article VIII protected the persons and property of "Mexicans now established in territories previously belonging to Mexico." It guaranteed them the right "to continue where they now reside, or to remove at any time to the Mexican Republic." The article went on to confer on those Mexicans who opted to stay all the rights and privileges of American citizenship. This included an explicit protection of "property of any kind," which was to be "inviolably respected."[42] This final guarantee meant nothing. Over the next half century, Mexicans throughout the border region were stripped of their land holdings through legal trickery and sometimes outright theft, invariably sanctioned by the courts.

Trist and his Mexican counterparts also pieced together a joint policy regarding a group that each side saw as the racial "other"—Native Americans. The original inhabitants of the border area stubbornly resisted every attempt to dominate them and fought Mexicans and Americans with equal vigor. Because their traditional home had been up until now entirely within Mexican territory, however, it was toward the Mexicans that Native Americans directed most of their enmity. At the negotiating table, the Mexicans demanded that the United States take appropriate steps to keep the ceded lands on its side from becoming sanctuaries from which cross-border raids could be launched. Thus, Article XI pledged the United States government to do all it could to deny Native Americans use of the border as a staging ground. Knowing the United States' traditional contempt for the culture and rights of Native Americans and the long history of dispossession and resettlement in the north, the Mexicans also demanded that any Native group pushed out of its lands above the border not be allowed to migrate south of it. Mexico did not relish the notion of becoming a dumping ground for its neighbor's ethnic problems. Yet despite Article XI's stipulations, the United States did little to prevent Native American attacks across the international boundary. That task fell to the Mexican and American border folk themselves, working in concert to ensure peace and security, often in the face of inaction and indifference on the parts of both national governments.

With that matter settled and a one-time payment of $15 million promised by the United States, the negotiations came to a conclusion. On February 2, 1848, Nicholas Trist, who had ignored an order from President Polk to return home without a treaty so that the American demands could be reformulated, signed the finished document for the United States; Luis G. Cuevas, Bernardo Couto, and Miguel Atristain did likewise for the Mexican Republic. Satisfied with their work, the delegates knew that the difficult part—ratification—lay ahead. The peace settlement would have to be taken to Washington and Mexico

City and presented to lawmakers in both capitals for what promised to be contentious debates.

The United States Senate took up the treaty first. Its debate began on February 28 and went on for 11 grueling days, during which time the growing rift between the North and South over the issue of slavery became painfully apparent. Americans had already become accustomed to drawing lines in an effort to satisfy both supporters and opponents of the South's "peculiar institution." The Mason-Dixon Line, which already served as the de facto (unofficial but generally recognized) border between freedom and slavery in the United States, had been extended to the edge of Mexican territory by the Missouri Compromise only 28 years earlier. Now, legislators from both sections had to consider yet another arbitrary boundary in terms of its impact on the North–South balance of political power and social influence.

Daniel Webster led the opposition to ratification, claiming that the acquisition of so much land handed the South an unprecedented opportunity to expand slavery across the continent. His followers even tried to insert a prohibition of slavery in the ceded territories into the document's text in words very similar to those used in 1846 by Pennsylvania Congressman David Wilmot. When the war began, Wilmot had lobbied for a total ban on slavery in any and all land gained during the war with Mexico. He failed then, and the Northern attempt to repackage his proposal met no better luck.

Southern senators, under the direction of Jefferson Davis of Mississippi, who later guided the Southern states out of the Union and into the Confederacy during the Civil War, and Texan Sam Houston, opposed the Treaty of Guadalupe Hidalgo for precisely the opposite reason. These slavery advocates argued that not enough territorial concessions had been wrung out of the Mexicans. Houston, in fact, wanted to grab all of Mexico to the city of Vera Cruz! Davis, slightly less ambitious, argued for the inclusion of all six Mexican border states in any deal.

Neither extreme, North or South, carried the day in the end. The majority of senators gave the president his treaty as it was,

Many Mexicans, including future president Benito Juárez, vehemently opposed the Treaty of Guadalupe Hidalgo and Mexico's surrender of territory to the United States. However, in 1848, the Mexican legislature voted in favor of the treaty and the border between Mexico and the United States was made official.

with the exception of one article. The Senate voted for ratification on March 10, 1848, by a vote of 38–14. The vast emptiness of the West to the pounding surf of the Pacific became American territory as far as the United States was concerned. The focus now shifted to Mexico City.

The Mexican congress opened its treaty debate on May 7, 1848. Opposition to ratification was immediate and impassioned. Closing ranks behind Manuel Rejón, opponents called for a flat rejection of the agreement's provisions. Mexico, they argued, surrendered too much in terms of both sovereignty and territory. Some, such as Rejón himself and future president Benito Juárez, went so far as to threaten renewed hostilities if the treaty passed. Juárez pronounced himself in favor of guerrilla warfare against American forces along the border, with the aim of driving out the foreign occupiers. Rejón's position was clear: The treaty as it had been written represented the first step toward the collapse of Mexican independence. What the United States could not do through war, erase Mexico as a sovereign state, it intended to accomplish through this piece of paper. Rejón predicted the end of Mexico if the government gained ratification of the treaty: "The treaty is our sentence of death," he warned.[43] Rejón also questioned the government's authority to make such a treaty in the first place. The Mexican representatives had no right to give up an inch of Mexican soil, let alone surrender California, the heart of Mexico's frontier patrimony, which Rejón referred to as "our priceless flower."[44] Priceless indeed, to a point not even the treaty opponents could have imagined. Millions of dollars worth of gold would soon flow out of the port of San Francisco. In conclusion, Rejón claimed that he could adjust to military defeat but never to Mexico's dismemberment.

The treaty's supporters argued their case with similar conviction and vehemence. They reminded the congress that many Americans, in particular Southern slave owners, had sought to take most, if not all, of Mexico in the event of an American victory during the war. These expansionists, treaty proponents contended, had not gone away and eagerly awaited the slimmest pretext to annex more Mexican land. The treaty, however flawed, offered the only hope for the survival of the republic.

The debates in Mexico City raged for nine tumultuous days. At one point, the arguments became so bitter and the rhetoric so heated that the states of Coahuila and Tamaulipas vowed never to accept the treaty, regardless of the outcome of the congress's vote for ratification. Oaxaca's governor, Benito Juárez, promised, that his state would fight the Americans single-handedly rather than give in to such an insult to Mexican sovereignty and honor. Several states, including Chihuahua and Jalisco, issued similar threats. One army general stationed outside Aguascalientes took his protest one step further by occupying the town and predicting a military coup if the congress voted to ratify the treaty. Despite all the insults, posturing, and dire pronouncements, when the vote was finally taken and the ballots counted, Mexico's legislature voted 51–34 in favor of the treaty as presented; three days later, the Senate did the same by a margin of 33–4.

By spring 1848, the frontier became a border, a line arbitrarily drawn through the heart of a place just beginning to show its promise. The two national governments etched their differences

THE REST OF THE TREATY

The major provisions of the Treaty of Guadalupe Hidalgo concerned the borderline, trade, and Mexican status in the ceded territories, but the document also touched on many other issues. Special arrangements for troop disengagement after the cease-fire outlined in Articles III and IV required a prompt American pullout from all occupied areas, an end to any current blockades of Mexican ports, and the immediate evacuation of Mexico City by Scott's army. Article III, interestingly enough, made the Mexicans responsible for the behavior of American troops during their withdrawal by demanding that the Mexican government ensure that the exit be made "convenient for the troops" by "promoting a good understanding between them and the [local] inhabitants."* This obligation carried greater weight, given the calls for guerrilla warfare emanating from states throughout Mexico. The treaty also called for free American access to Mexican ports in the Sea of Cortez, especially near the mouth of the Colorado River (Article VI) and for a guarantee against Apache slave raids into Mexico (Article XI). With the American slave states so near, it seems that Mexican authorities were seriously concerned about Apaches slipping into their country, kidnapping Mexicans, and selling them in the United States. They did not want to see Mexicans laboring beside black slaves on Southern plantations.

* Griswold, *Treaty of Guadalupe Hidalgo*, p. 185.

and the remedy to their problems on a region ready to cultivate a bicultural character and way of life. An artificial boundary, crafted and agreed on by outsiders, had been imposed; this boundary would fundamentally alter the evolution of local development. Interdependence remained a fact for the border community, but now it became hopelessly encrusted with national issues and interests.

Mexican and American border folk faced each other on different terms after the Treaty of Guadalupe Hidalgo. Events compelled them to view one another through a national prism that distorted local relationships. The people on the border confronted a paradox in which each was simultaneously familiar and foreign. The treaty settled old problems for Washington and Mexico City but generated new ones for the border community. The old social model of interaction became obsolete with the imposition of a dividing line; novel constructs and assumptions would have to be tested. What it all might come to, no one knew.

6

Boom Times— The Border, 1850–1910

As American and Mexican legislators debated the relative merits of the Treaty of Guadalupe Hidalgo, San Francisco and other towns in northern California released news that gold had been discovered along the American River. Within a year, reports of the gold strike reached the East, triggering the greatest internal migration in American history. To have a mule, a pan, and a small piece of muddy riverbank suddenly became an aspiration for farmers, craftsmen, and clerks who had never seen and probably never would see a golden nugget. In Texas, the rush began somewhat later and involved cattle, not gold. The rise of the cattle business in the Lone Star State occurred during the brief period between the mid-1860s and the 1880s. Busy ranches, teeming herds of cattle, and long drives that ended ultimately at the slaughterhouses of Chicago brought wealth and fame to Texas.

Enshrined in popular fiction and film, the mythical West of California miners, Texas cowhands, and dusty Mexican banditos overshadows the very real place that extended from the Rio Grande to the Pacific, reached as far north as San Francisco, and dipped southward, encompassing the six Mexican border states. In this vast tract of land, life changed dramatically after peace. Gold and cattle certainly brought riches to many Westerners and their Mexican counterparts, but they reflected only one aspect of a far more complex economic boom that transformed the border in many ways.

The local community that resumed its evolution along the border after 1848 enjoyed unprecedented prosperity. Extensive mining operations, concentrating on the extraction of ores of much greater long-term significance than gold, gouged out profits from the Sonoran desert. Farms and commercial agriculture brought millions of acres under the plow, producing huge surpluses of high-quality grain. Railroads transported this bounty out of the region and linked the population centers that began to sprout up as newcomers arrived to take advantage of opportunities for gain. Along with this economic development came new problems, which were either directly or indirectly

Following the enactment of the Treaty of Guadalupe Hidalgo, many communities in the West and along the border enjoyed unprecedented wealth. The most legendary economic developments in the region were the gold rush in California and cattle herding, which brought fame and wealth to Texas. The Long Horn cattle seen in this engraving by Edward Rapier are being driven to a cattle rendezvous in Dodge City.

attributable to the international boundary. Social and cultural tensions arose as people tried to discern exactly what the border meant to them and·their future. Before this sort of individual and collective reckoning could take place, people needed to know exactly where the border was. Simple though it might sound, it took five years to determine and adjust the precise location of the border.

Drawing a line on a map was one thing; finding it on the ground, it seemed, was quite another. Although the Treaty of Guadalupe Hidalgo left no doubt that a revised international boundary followed a river path to the Pacific, no one was certain where the border ran in the empty desert flats and desolate scrublands that sat between the area's major rivers. Someone had to trace out the border by actually surveying the line from one end to the other. This task fell to a joint commission, as prescribed in

Article V of the treaty. The commission was responsible for locating the border both in the places where it followed the Rio Grande and Gila rivers and where it shot across the featureless Sonoran desert and the dry plains of Baja California. Given the size of the area in question, its barrenness, and the harsh extremes of its climate, the job promised little money and much hardship. Finding a survey team was difficult; hiring a commissioner proved almost impossible.

It took three attempts before a willing and, more importantly, competent American candidate was interviewed and selected. His name was John Russell Bartlett, a Rhode Island bookseller seeking adventure and travel, driven by what one historian has characterized as "lifelong restlessness" and "innate inquisitiveness."[45] The Mexicans chose to appoint a general, Pedro Garcia Conde, to lead their part of the team. Both men turned out to be adept at political maneuvering, and each constantly sought to gain the advantage for his country. Bartlett, however, went one step further by actually accompanying the joint survey party on its trip. Bartlett's impetuousness won him the chore of settling occasionally violent disagreements among team members. During the trip, he endured heat, cold, and a serious illness that confined him to a bed in Mexico for months. Bartlett and Garcia Conde became fast friends despite constant haggling over major and minor points associated with the survey. At last, in December 1853, the joint commission finished its work.

The border, following the Treaty of Guadalupe Hidalgo's terms as faithfully as possible, ran along the Rio Grande as far as El Paso before crossing over to the Gila River. The boundary continued along the Gila to the Colorado River and from there shot straight to the Pacific Ocean just south of San Diego. The line had been set as agreed on, pending one "modification" of special interest to the United States.

While the survey team was still at work, the United States moved to acquire the land known as La Mesilla, which lay due south of the Gila River. The international boundary as decided at Guadalupe Hidalgo had not factored in a direct route for any future transcontinental railroad, nor had it taken into account how bitterly such a route would be debated by Northern and Southern politicians. The controversy over slavery spilled over into discussions of how to connect the East with California. It was taken for granted that the commercial Northeast would eventually build its own line, connecting Eastern factories to markets in the West, but the South wanted its share as well. Southern farmers needed a railroad as badly as did Northern merchants, and a Southern connection might also facilitate the expansion of slavery into the Southwest.

An essentially Southern railroad was crucial to the region's prospects for growth, but the corridor through which trains

THE CHAMIZAL CONTROVERSY

One of the oldest and most frustrating questions following the border settlement in the Treaty of Guadalupe Hidalgo concerned a 600-acre stretch of riverbank near El Paso known as the Chamizal. The treaty's authors believed that no portion of the new border would be as stable as the venerable Rio Grande. Diplomats first and foremost, those at Guadalupe Hidalgo knew nothing of hydrology and the dynamics of waterways. They did not know that rivers could and often did unexpectedly change course. The Rio Grande did this in the Chamizal. The river swung repeatedly first to the north and then to the south of the agreed on boundary line. In 1864, the great river shifted southward, dragging a large chunk of the Mexican state of Chihuahua technically into the United States. Mexico protested, but not too vigorously, prompting the United States to refrain from taking any action that might in any way be construed as annexation. The matter was not settled formally until 1963, although an agreement pertaining to a similar river dispute farther down the Rio Grande was signed in 1884. The nearly century-long lag between the beginning of the Chamizal controversy and its resolution is explained best by historian David Lorey: While of deep concern to the local community, neither national government "assigned the matter a high priority."*

* Lorey, *U.S.-Mexican Border*, p. 154.

The key to this new economy was a careful combination of American money and Mexican resources, and the chief resource lay underground. Between 1870 and 1900, mining became the most important economic activity along the border, especially in the Mexican states of Sonora and Chihuahua. Mining operations, run with American money invested by companies and individuals, grew exponentially. By the first years of the twentieth century, Americans owned half of the companies pulling gold, silver, lead, and copper out of the Mexican ground. As the number and productivity of northern Mexican mines increased, so did the general prosperity of the border region. Oil exploration and drilling, made profitable with the invention of the internal combustion engine, joined metals as staples of the Mexican economy in the 1890s. Manufacturing also grew. Mexican plants, often located conveniently close to the international boundary, turned out a wide variety of valuable products, from steel and bricks to clothing and cigarettes, ready for sale in Mexico or export to the United States.

All of this bounty made its way north and south of the border on railroads that not only crisscrossed the American Southwest and Mexican north but also radiated outward toward the national centers. Within 30 years, the border was connected by rail to markets and cities throughout the United States and Mexico, facilitating the movement of goods and people to a degree never before experienced. More important, however, the border community itself became thoroughly integrated and bound together as one economic and social entity. The northern Mexican states, for example, laid claim to more than 6,500 miles of railroad tracks, more than half of all the railroad tracks in Mexico by 1900, but most of those tracks led to American border towns. In fact, it has been convincingly argued that, "The railroad tied Mexican communities more closely to the United States than to the Mexican interior."[48]

Railroad transportation and industrial wealth invariably led to population growth and urbanization. After almost 300 years, la frontera finally had the most precious resource of all—people.

Northern Mexico, in particular, filled up at an impressive rate. Dusty towns became relatively instant cities. Salinas, Coahuila, grew from 778 residents in 1877 to 15,000 within 23 years; Nuevo Laredo, Tamaulipas, went from a meager population of 1,200 to 9,000 during the same period. Nogales, Sonora, however, stands out—in less than three decades, it exploded from a scant 10 residents to nearly 9,000.[49] Across the artificial borderline, the story followed a similar script. Los Angeles shot up to more than 100,000 in 1900 from a mere 6,000 inhabitants 30 years earlier; San Antonio swelled to 53,000 from 12,000.[50] Mexicans and Americans from far beyond the border region flocked to the new El Dorado along the international boundary.

American investment and Mexican resources energized the border economy, but the political impetus for growth came from Mexico. The rise of Porfirio Díaz to the Mexican presidency in 1876 heralded a new era for Mexico and the border community. The long years of his rule, 1876–1910, saw a dynamic Mexico grow in power and wealth. Through a program known as "Order and Progress," Díaz encouraged long-term investment, economic integration, and financial stability. His government centralized authority to an extent never before witnessed in Mexico. Perhaps Díaz's contribution came in the form of North America's first free-trade zone, the *Zona Libre*, within the border region, which, after 1885, allowed for untaxed trade along and across the boundary line.

Mexico and the United States cooperated on a massive and international scale between 1850 and 1910. This cooperation resulted in extensive economic integration and success. Collaboration on a local level gave similar results but also fostered a renewed sense of community. Throughout the region, cultural exchange and blending grew more pronounced. Mexicans and Americans passed one another as they crossed the border in search of jobs or business opportunities. In places like Sonora and Arizona, customs traversed the dividing line as well. Few could miss the cumulative effect of such interaction. The Nogales (Arizona) *Oasis*, when discussing its Mexican sister city of the same name, noted, "We speak of the two towns as one, for they really are such, being divided by an imaginary line only."[51] Business owners in the same town made clear their conviction that even when trouble did arise, local problems demanded local solutions. In 1893, the Americans sent a letter to the Nogales (Sonora) city council stating, "Petty international questions are almost unavoidable owing to our peculiar international situation. We believe that such questions, not affecting the dignity of either nation can best be settled among ourselves without involving our respective governments in vexatious international controversies."[52] Neither side wanted any more outside interference in local matters than was absolutely necessary or unavoidable.

By 1910, the border had come into its own. For all its internal tension and strife, the region had become central to the national economies of both Mexico and the United States. A rough equilibrium had been achieved whereby the center exerted just as much influence as the periphery would tolerate. The border had been born and continued to grow. A new century would test its resilience.

7

Revolution and Intervention

Between the signing of the Treaty of Guadalupe Hidalgo and Mexico's descent into revolution, the border was literally and figuratively redefined. Decades of social upheaval and economic change fueled a transformation of the border region. Locally, it remained a place of fluid interaction between people and cultures, characterized by alternating periods of harmony and discord, cooperation and conflict. To the central governments, however, the border rematerialized in the late nineteenth century as an imaginary fortress. The Treaty of Guadalupe Hidalgo and its corollary, the Treaty of Mesilla, molded a space interpreted ideologically by both Mexico and the United States as being a barrier against an ever-encroaching "other." The international boundary's physical integrity (soundness) and local validity were mitigated by the boom years of rapid growth and prosperity that began in 1850, but the illusion of the border's capacity to separate the inseparable had not weakened in the national capitals.

The line so carefully crafted in 1848, however abstract on a local level, continued to divide wary national centers. Guided as it was by interests and agendas divorced from the reality of border life, the border involved the governments in a national symbolic system guaranteed to encourage suspicion and mutual misunderstanding. Simply put, as the borderline failed for the local community between 1850 and 1910, it came into much sharper focus nationally. The centers saw more clearly something the periphery increasingly ignored—an illusion called the border.

The treaties of Guadalupe Hidalgo and Mesilla split the border community into two halves, each subordinated to its respective national center. Consequently, border folk were compelled to assume national identities that expressed themselves in contrived oppositional roles as "Mexicans" and "Americans." Forced to read from scripts that exaggerated local distinctions, the local community nonetheless struggled to retain an autonomous character through the late nineteenth century and into the first decades of the twentieth. This chore became tougher as the border became an essential component of two different national economies, societies, and political orders.

The border community's effort to remain cohesive and cooperative became much more difficult as U.S.-Mexican relations entered a period of bitter conflict and international estrangement. Antagonism grew between the national governments; this distorted local relations and undermined institutions all along the border. In consequence, the border community, interdependent as ever, now had to adjust to an imaginary arena for daily life that emphasized conflict and "otherness" to a greater degree than perhaps at any other time in Mexican-American history. Trouble lay ahead.

In the early 1900s, the era of the "imperial presidency," the label attached to the rapid expansion of executive powers under the American President Theodore Roosevelt, had just gotten under way in the United States as its older counterpart in Mexico began to crumble. Notwithstanding its contribution to Mexican prosperity and modernization, Díaz's "Order and Progress" program was a spent force. Along with wealth and stability, the program brought rigid political centralization and heavy-handed management of the economy. This, in turn, produced commercial and administrative structures characterized by inflexibility and reactionary responses to even normal, gradual change, let alone the convulsions of economic depression and social unrest.

Mexico's vulnerability to such a system became clear in 1907. Drought struck large portions of the republic, causing widespread crop failures, followed by the inevitable food shortages. Food prices at local markets skyrocketed. Problems in the agricultural sector soon spread throughout the Mexican economy, accelerated by a coincidental recession in the United States. Unemployment rose sharply, wages fell, and mining operations and manufacturing came to a virtual standstill. The trickle of Mexicans across the border became a torrent: In 1908 alone, 60,000 to 100,000 Mexicans immigrated to the United States. One year later, Mexicans made up 7 percent of all mineworkers and 13 percent of laborers in American smelting plants. By

1912, railroads reported that the majority of their workers were Mexican immigrants.[53] As wages and prices collapsed at home, Mexicans left for the United States. Mexico's economy ground to a halt.

Mexicans, told by their government that the troubles would be temporary, began to grumble and demand change, none more loudly than those in the six border states where boom times had indisputably come to an end. The border suffered more profoundly and extensively than any other part of Mexico. The population had grown faster there, and the economy, although robust, proved less resilient and more vulnerable to disruption. In other words, these states endured disproportionate hardships after 1907. It was no great surprise to anyone that the most serious challenge to Díaz's programs, and his rule, came from the border community.

The first calls for reform came from Francisco Madero, a native son of the border. Heir to his family's fortunes, which was built through extensive involvement in mining, Madero was born and raised in Coahuila. Although his physical needs could be met easily on the family estate, Madero's parents felt compelled to send him abroad for schooling, first in California and then in France. His sojourn in Europe exposed the young Mexican to the ideology of radical democracy. On his return home, Madero began to construct a revolutionary vision of Mexico's future that focused on peace and prosperity for all within a truly representative and responsive political system.

Madero's near obsession with fairness and equity in the economy and politics sprang from his border mentality. His worldview had been shaped by the dual imperatives of economic progress and genuine federalism (distribution of power between authority and constituents), which translated for Madero into a balance between center and periphery. This type of construct, informed by border assumptions about relationships within a republic, was alien to Díaz's thinking. The president possessed neither the inclination nor the intellectual agility to wrap his mind around ideas that did not assume a national orientation

When Mexico began to suffer from economic and social problems after the turn of the twentieth century, Francisco Madero, a native of the border, was the first to call for reform. Madero, seen here, led a successful revolt against President Porfirio Díaz in 1911 and became president himself.

and firm central authority. For Díaz, all roads in the republic led to Mexico City. The tension and incompatibility between the viewpoints represented by the president and Madero led inevitably to revolution.

Initially, Madero and a host of other reformers hoped to challenge Díaz at the ballot box. The president's decision to step down in 1910 gave the reform camp an opportunity to take power and change Mexico. Díaz, always unpredictable, had other ideas: He announced his intention to continue in office. His opponents, Madero chief among them, felt they had no choice but to move outside the law; they opted for armed struggle, with the border native as their standard bearer. The northern states quickly lined up behind Madero, propelling him into the presidency in 1911.

Carrying an indelible border imprint, revolutionary activity was concentrated for the most part along the boundary with the United States. The burden of fighting for liberation, bearing up under the weight of war, fell heaviest on the border community, and it was from here that perhaps the most famous leader of the revolution—Doroteo Arango, better known as Francisco "Pancho" Villa—came.

An unemployed cattle hand and part-time petty bandit, Villa assumed command of a small revolutionary force drawn from among the border folk and began striking a series of blows against federal troops stationed throughout the north. Villa's bold, often reckless attacks against government troops sometimes took place very close to the international boundary and occasionally spilled over it. As a result, the border community endured a period of bloodshed and confusion that other parts of Mexico were spared. As in 1848, issues of national sovereignty, would be settled on its soil.

War, possible and probable, hung over Mexican-American relations. The Treaty of Guadalupe Hidalgo, although a peace treaty, thus forbade any future conflict between the republics. The treaty demanded the protection of trade and investments, outlined the humane treatment of prisoners of war, and even promised that churches, hospitals, schools, colleges, libraries, and "other establishments for charitable and beneficent purposes shall be respected."[54] What the treaty did not anticipate was revolutionary warfare within the bounds of one signatory crossing over into the territory of the other. On this point, the treaty fell silent just where the border community needed it to speak.

Madero's overthrow and assassination by General Victoriano Huerta in 1913 changed the course of the revolution. Madero's movement had been essentially political, but now the military aspect came to predominate. Villa, determined to conduct the rebellion in his own way, assumed command of all rebel forces along the border, a contingent that in 1914 was dubbed the Division del Norte (Division of the North). Without losing a moment's time, he went on the offensive against the *federales,* with spectacular success. Villa's triumphs gained him not only widespread notoriety on both sides of the border (so much so

THE REVOLUTION AS THEATER

The Mexican Revolution provided the backdrop for early efforts at documenting and dramatizing war on film. Although photographers had been a fixture on Civil War battlefields and in European war zones, their subjects had been exclusively military, and, partly because of the state of the art in the mid-nineteenth century, most of their work had been staged. The Mexican Revolution offered a unique opportunity not only to catch the action as it happened, but also to watch civilians as they watched the war and thus use the contest, especially the much-crossed border, as a metaphor for social and cultural differences. Throughout the fighting between 1910 and roughly 1920, photographers and even some early filmmakers used the border to convey a sense of national opposites. They literally used the border to express just how foreign, how "other," the other side was. The Rio Grande, for example, figured prominently in period photographs as a watery barrier that split the frame, marking it as a visual line of separation between the American spectators on one bank and the Mexican townspeople and revolutionaries on the other. Along those desert portions of the border that partitioned Arizona and Sonora, shots of streets down the middle of which the border ran served a similar purpose. Occasionally, the odd border marker, with its strange obelisk-like shape, turned up in pictures when neither river nor street was available. In these shots, representatives of the two nations and cultures, often soldiers from the two countries, were positioned on their respective sides for contrast. Regardless of the subject, though, the message sent by the photographs of the border and the war remained the same: The international boundary really did separate two distinct peoples and their realities, one stereotypically Mexican and one quintessentially American. The local community did not see it that way, but, as Claire Fox has pointed out, the border was portrayed in photographs, movies, and even postcards as if it were an accurate reflection of "the nations it divides. That is, developments on the border are perceived to be symptomatic of the overall status of U.S.-Mexico relations." As usual, however, "the importance of border events is presented from the point of view of national actors rather than local inhabitants."*

* Claire Fox, *The Fence and the River: Culture and Politics at the U.S.-Mexico Border.* Minneapolis: University of Minnesota Press, 1999, p. 69.

that the American film director D. W. Griffith made a semidocumentary film about the rebel commander's exploits) but also the enmity of fellow revolutionaries such as the ambitious Venustiano Carranza.

By 1915, a massive rift opened between Villa, leading his border army, and Carranza, who had maneuvered himself into power in Mexico City after the downfall of Huerta. The subsequent conduct of both men spoke volumes about the traditional center-periphery struggle in Mexico. Villa routinely seized property and resources belonging to the border elite, a group that owed its station in life and political power to the federal government, and redistributed it all. Profits from farmland Villa ordered sold went into a fund for the widows and orphans of his fallen soldiers. The commander and his closest allies pocketed their share of the wealth, of course, but Villa's generosity was remarkable, especially when one considers that the border recipients of that generosity had been so thoroughly ignored by the central government.

After occupying the capital of Chihuahua, for example, Villa took over a department store and doled out clothing and shoes to local residents and candy to their children. Later, he gave meat, milk, and bread to charities serving the state's poorest children. Villa ordered that meat and grain prices be kept at levels low enough to ensure that the working class could afford such necessities.[55]

Carranza, for his part, feared Villa's growing popularity. A former governor of Chihuahua himself, Carranza hoped to persuade the Mexican public to accept the legitimacy of his power and identify with the central government. Villa stood in his way. Carranza thus terminated his political support for his former comrade and cut off supplies set aside for the Division del Norte. Open warfare between the two groups soon broke out, with international implications.

The United States was neither unaffected nor sitting in passive observation as the conflict between Villa and Carranza erupted. The American portion of the local community braced itself for the intense Mexican infighting that followed the split in the rebel leadership. Border Americans knew that they would experience the subsequent power struggle firsthand. History proved them right: Some of the most important battles of the latter part of the revolution took place literally on their doorsteps.

Initially, the U.S. government took the border's integrity for granted. After all, both nations had promised to respect it "religiously." From a distance, the international boundary appeared far more imposing and formidable than it really was. Moreover, from their vantage point in Washington, American officials understood the border in solely national terms, as an aspect of relations between the two capitals. How the bold map line actually translated on the ground, in terms of geography and the local community, escaped them.

The Rio Grande was shallow, and it narrowed at some points to a stone's throw from bank to bank—not exactly the most impressive barrier. Through the desert, the line was nothing more than an occasional stone marker or wooden post. In one particular location, Nogales, Arizona/Sonora (Mexico), the border ran down the middle of a street shared and traversed by Mexicans and Americans on a daily basis. Historians have remarked that, despite the border, "Nogales, Arizona, and Nogales, Sonora, are physically one town." Given that fact, the boundary line had no practical value or impact once the fighting began. That Americans were in close proximity to the fighting meant that "bullets from the Mexican side continually fell on the American side."[56]

Americans living in border towns grew used to the sound of gunfire during the Mexican Revolution. As early as 1913, Arizonans in Nogales found themselves closer than they liked to a battle between troops loyal to Villa and men serving Carranza. During the combat, as stray bullets shattered windows and nerves on the American side, the local U.S. Army commander became convinced that the fighting would spill across the street into the United States. His remedy was simple: He ordered his soldiers to mount a machine gun on a hill overlooking the borderline and to open fire on any Mexican combatants who dared to cross it. None did, except for 250 Carrancistas who opted to surrender to the Americans rather than take their chances with the Villistas.[57]

Similar scenes played themselves out all along the border. In December 1914, 41 residents of Naco, Arizona, died in the crossfire during a skirmish between elements of the Villa and Carranza armies. Mexican snipers shot and killed two Americans who had been clearly on the U.S. side of the boundary, a brazen violation of international law. This time, loss of life was too great to be ignored; Naco attracted the attention of the central government. In frustration and anger, President Woodrow Wilson commanded the army chief of staff to "go down [to the border] and drive those armies away."[58] The general did his best, but the border remained a dangerous place. During the battle of Agua Prieta, October–November 1915, the fighting became so intense that units of no fewer than seven different U.S. Army regiments dug and occupied trenches around the town of Douglas, Arizona, in an effort to defend it against a Mexican incursion.[59]

The Mexican Revolution crossed the border with frightening regularity, highlighting the fictional quality of the international boundary line that the Treaty of Guadalupe Hidalgo had established to guarantee "peace and good neighbourship" for eternity.[60] The imagined power of the border to separate the local community melted away in the face of real warfare that affected both sides. Lines that seemed so clear and impermeable in Washington and Mexico City blurred and suddenly became porous.

The most notorious event showing just how porous these lines were took place in March 1916. In an effort to punish the United States for supporting Carranza, and perhaps to provoke an imprudently excessive reply from the Americans, 500 Villistas crossed the border and raided the town of Columbus, New Mexico, killing 14 U.S. soldiers and 10 civilians.

Public opinion demanded a response to the Columbus raid, as Mexican rebels repeatedly violated the border, and the number

Pancho Villa was the most famous leader of the Mexican Revolution, which often crossed the border into the United States. Several Americans were killed in the crossfire, and General John Pershing tried to hunt down Villa for almost a year, until America's entry into World War I ended the expedition. In this photograph taken at the border in Arizona in 1916, Pancho Villa stands between General Alvaro Obregon and General John J. Pershing during a friendly meeting.

of civilian casualties rose. The discovery of an ill-conceived plot to kill white border inhabitants, hatched by a small group of fanatics and called the Plan de San Diego, only aggravated matters. Combined with the general economic chaos caused by the revolution and the insult of the Columbus raid, the Plan de San Diego proved to be the last straw. Despite the pledge in Article XXI of the Treaty of Guadalupe Hidalgo to settle any "disagreement [that] should hereafter arise between the Governments of the two Republics,"[61] in March 1916, President Wilson ordered General John Pershing to cross into Mexican territory with an expeditionary force and hunt down Villa.

The general and his more than 6,000 men tried to do just that, without much success. For almost a year, Pershing chased Villa around northern Mexico, until events in Europe, where America's entry into World War I seemed imminent. Strained relations with the Carranza government over the continued presence of American troops on Mexican soil brought an end to the expedition. Notwithstanding the interception by American intelligence of the Zimmerman Telegram (a secret communication between Germany and its consulate in Mexico City hinting at possible German aid in the event that Mexico chose to reclaim what it had lost at Guadalupe Hidalgo), the tension along the border abated. Sporadic fighting took place in northern Mexico for a few years, but by 1920 the revolution was over.

On a national level, the Mexican Revolution emphasized the fictional qualities of the border and the flimsiness of the Treaty of Guadalupe Hidalgo's most important provisions. Despite the "safeguards" against conflict built into the treaty, the events of the revolutionary years poisoned international relations more thoroughly than anything else since 1846. The Columbus raid and the Pershing expedition wasted a surplus of goodwill between the central governments that had been built up painstakingly over the course of 50 years. Locally, the prosperity enjoyed by the American border states had evaporated and the Mexican economy shattered. Trade, commerce, and industry ceased to function in any real way. Farms were destroyed, mines shut down, and people on both sides of the border were murdered and terrorized.

With the revolution, the local order that had been so carefully constructed came crashing down. Only as Mexican politics stabilized and the United States became distracted by the war in Europe could the border community begin to sift through the debris of war and begin the process of social and economic reconstruction.

8

Prohibition and Depression on the Border

The upheaval of the Mexican Revolution propelled the border community into the twentieth century and fundamentally altered international relations between the United States and Mexico. Both national governments came to understand their interdependence and to realize the importance of the border society and local economy that their actions had so completely disrupted. The governments in Washington and Mexico City, distracted by more "important" matters, stood by as the border community recovered from war and reestablished patterns of cooperation and conflict that had traditionally transcended the boundary line. The centers watched as the periphery revived modes of living and interacting that had been evolving since 1848.

The Treaty of Guadalupe Hidalgo had envisioned an integrated trading partnership between Mexico and the United States in which national needs were met and national interests protected. At the same time, the treaty never anticipated the development of a regional border economy fully integrated into the larger national ones while operating semi-independently and primarily benefiting the local community. Just such a model emerged in the 1920s.

Even before the end of World War I, the border began to stir with renewed activity. Mexico struggled to reconstruct its civil and political society and the United States fought in its first major war overseas; at the same time, however, the foundation was being laid for a regional border economy wherein Mexican labor and immigrants moving northward passed American money and tourists flowing southward. The old connections of trade and industrial commerce had been severed by the revolution, but these connections had been replaced by new ones that reflected an economic equation in which progress resulted from the Mexican willingness to export its greatest resource, hardworking people, and from American eagerness to invest large sums in enterprises freed from the constraints of a marketplace governed by rules made in Washington, D.C.

Migration signaled the advent of this arrangement. What

After the revolution, Mexican immigrants flooded into the United States. Immigration regulations were strict during the 1920s and 1930s, and immigrants faced barriers such as literacy tests and head taxes. This Mexican man is being searched by a U.S. customs inspector near the border in Juarez, Mexico.

started as a trickle during the revolution became a flood of Mexican immigrants afterward. During the second decade of the twentieth century, particularly the later years, 10 percent of Mexico's total population, including 628,000 temporary workers, moved to the United States.[62] These people, looking for work and a chance to rebuild lives pulled apart by war, entered into a Southwestern American economy shifting toward agriculture. The amount of land under cultivation in California, Arizona, New Mexico, and Texas increased at a steady pace, as did the corresponding need for reliable, plentiful labor. Seemingly in an instant, American growers became dependent on Mexican workers.

Politically, this situation led to calls for a lowering of the barriers to immigration that became popular during World War I and rose to new heights in the early 1920s. The Immigration Act of 1917, for example, placed significant burdens, including a literacy test and a head tax, on people attempting to enter the United States from Mexico. The American government was determined to dissuade Mexicans from immigrating and set suitably unreasonable standards for legal entry. Nationalists and racists took comfort in the knowledge that Mexicans would have a difficult time crossing the international boundary, but border farmers did not. The impulse toward exclusion figured much more prominently in the worldview of those Americans who neither lived nor worked within the local community; border folk knew only inclusion, however erratic.

The more stringent rules threatened to create a dangerous labor shortage. No sooner had the act gone into effect than the U.S. border growers lobbied the central government for relaxation of those rules. Most of the larger agricultural operations protested along the lines of the argument presented by one border cotton company executive, who wrote to President Wilson saying, "Personally, I believe that the Mexican laborers are the solution to our common labor problem in this country. Many of their people are here, this was once part of their country, and they can and they will do the work.... I personally find them, especially those with families, to be appreciative of fair treatment and to be deserving of it."[63] After similar testimony from farm operators throughout the Southwest, Congress finally relented and lifted the test and tax requirements. When it came to the infamous Immigration Act of 1924, crafted explicitly to reduce "nonwhite" immigration, American growers scored an even more surprising victory in Washington—Congress excluded Mexicans altogether from the strict quota system set up in the legislation. No other significant obstacle to Mexican immigration would be raised until 1965.

In opening a wide portal connecting the two halves of the local community, the federal government merely recognized a fact well known along the border: Mexican labor was essential to the entire region's economic growth and prosperity. American growers could increase production and lower costs, and Mexicans gained the steady work and reliable incomes that accelerated postrevolutionary reconstruction. National as well as local ends were being served. Acknowledging, however indirectly, the borderless nature of the local community and giving legitimacy to a practice that would continue anyway went a long way toward healing the international wound opened by the Mexican rebel raids and the Pershing expedition. In the end, according to David Lorey, the "great need for inexpensive labor in the U.S. border region and the desire to improve relations [had] compelled the United States to allow Mexicans to continue entering the country with relative ease."[64]

Labor and agriculture combined to revitalize the border. Other opportunities for cooperation, however, presented themselves in unexpected ways during the 1920s. Following decades of anti-"booze" agitation and crusades aimed at rejuvenating a United States believed by many to be in a state of moral decay, Congress passed the Eighteenth Amendment to the Constitution, banning the manufacturing, sale, and consumption of alcohol. America went dry. Not only did bars and restaurants experience the pinch of going without liquor, but a wide spectrum of "immoral" forms of entertainment, from race tracks and casinos to dance halls, sat by helplessly as their patrons and profits disappeared. The United States, at least officially, turned its back on alcohol and just about everything associated with it.

The United States seemed to have found some value in denying the allure and attendant pleasures of drinking, but Mexico did not. Mexican cities such as Tijuana and Ciudad Juárez announced to a parched America that they were open for business. These and other places became attractive not only to legitimate tourists seeking a safe haven where they could slake their thirst but also to the new American criminal underground that supplied smuggled liquor to American consumers in cities and towns far from the border.

Overnight, a popular image of Mexican vice and loose morals took hold in the United States, titillating some people and offending others. Among the latter were racist social advocates, conservative politicians, and mainstream Protestant religious groups such as the Methodist Church. In 1920, the Church's Board of Temperance, Prohibition, and Public Morals lamented the fact that "Everything goes at Tia Juana [sic].... There are scores of gambling devices, long drinking bars, dance halls, hop joints, cribs for prostitutes, cock fights, dog fights, bull fights.... The town is a mecca of prostitutes, booze sellers, gamblers and other American vermin."[65]

No doubt, after World War I, crime and illicit entertainment represented growth industries along the Mexican side of the border, but the real engine for economic expansion was everyday tourism. One contemporary estimate of border crossings by motorists from the East driving to California claimed that at least three-quarters of all transcontinental travelers stopped over in Mexico. Cíudad Juárez and Tijuana were favorite spots. Tijuana, for instance, drew so many American visitors on July 4, 1920, that gasoline stations in San Diego emptied their pumps. The city literally ran out of gas as 65,000 people in cars went south of the border.[66]

Much as those from San Diego viewed Tijuana, people in El Paso looked at Juárez as the spark plug of the city's economy. In 1921, a hotel executive argued that, "Juárez is our greatest asset and we are just beginning to realize it."[67] A consultant to the city of El Paso urged the planning department to cultivate closer ties with Ciudad Juárez. "It is in El Paso's interest," he emphasized, "to cooperate most energetically with the people of Juárez and the government of Mexico to promote legitimate development of the Mexican city."[68]

Americans and their dollars crossed the border in vast numbers during the 1920s, passing an equally impressive stream of Mexicans heading in the opposite direction seeking jobs. Traditional interdependence and cooperation had been reestablished after the turmoil of the revolution. Differences and dis-

BORDER ALLURE—THEN AND NOW

Mexico, the border cities in particular, drew hundreds of thousands of American visitors during the 1920s. Some came to sightsee, others to do business, but most crossed the border simply to party. Eighty years later, little has changed. Americans, now mostly underage high-school and college students, still cross the border daily, or nightly as the case may be, to slake their thirst on inexpensive Mexican beer and tequila. Prime party spots include Tijuana and Matamoros. Of the latter, one good-time aficionado commented, "Living right on the border of the United States and Mexico proved to be a wondrous thing for the underaged in Brownsville. Just a few minutes away was a town full of discos and bars where anyone who could see over the bar could get a drink."* During the 2002 Labor Day weekend, Tijuana attracted so many young Americans looking to drink that a National City, California, advisory group put together a leaflet campaign in San Diego "to combat underage drinking and prevent people from driving home drunk after partying in Mexico."** The group hoped to reduce the flow of drinkers crossing southward at night and the number of drunks staggering northward the next morning. Echoing the complaints of an earlier era, the group argued that "aggressive marketing practices lure thousands of high-school, college, and university students from across the region to drink in Tijuana, Mexico ... which translates into an increase in the number of alcohol-related problems at the border."*** In conscious imitation of the Border Patrol, the organization called its project Operation Safe Crossing.

---

* "Partying in Matamoros, Mexico," http://www.maelstrom.org/mischief/history/mex.html. Online. 10 November 2003.

** "Law Enforcement to Crack Down on Youth Partying in Tijuana Over Labor Day Weekend." Institute for Public Strategies, www.publicstrategies.org. 28 August 2002. Online. 10 November 2003.

*** Ibid.

agreements remained a fact of life, but once more, as in the past, these were locally oriented, as was the prosperity enjoyed by the border community. Though the national governments on both sides of the line might not have noticed, the border community had been revived and forward momentum regained—that is, until a certain Tuesday in 1929.

Far from the border, in New York City, banks and corporate investors undid everything the border community had worked so hard to accomplish. The collapse of the American stock market on Tuesday, October 29, 1929, brought a halt to the redevelopment of the border. As the national economies of the United States and Mexico staggered and fell, the border economy entered what local Mexicans called *La Crisis*.

It took almost a year for the Great Depression to make its way south and west from its source in New York. When the wave of financial disaster finally struck, the local community responded much as it had during the dark days of the revolution: with confusion, followed by angry recriminations, and conflict. El Paso and Ciudad Juárez, for example, were hit equally hard, but soon turned on one another. Residents of El Paso developed an acute case of protectionism and came to believe that their Mexican neighbors, however inadvertently, were aggravating the hard times. The American public had little sympathy for Mexican workers who competed for jobs in an economy that had experienced a 21 percent decline in manufacturing and 63 percent drop in the factory work force.[69]

Mexican labor, it was said, made the problems of a collapsing economy worse. One El Paso newspaper expressed the prevailing mood:

> If these aliens did not come over ... many American citizens that are now walking the streets, would be earning a living for themselves, their wives, and babies.... We do not blame these Mexican workers. We have no malice toward them, but self-preservation is the first law of nature, and our first duty is to our own—those for whom we are responsible....[70]

Instead of looking outside the border region for the origins of their troubles, the local community accused its own.

Border relations everywhere, from Brownsville, Texas, to San Diego, California, similarly deteriorated. In Tucson, Arizona, for instance, as the city's businesses closed and banks failed, American employers tried to remedy the situation by laying off their Mexican workers. Affected disproportionately by the firings and dismissals, Mexicans felt the economic impact of widespread unemployment and a 50 percent reduction in income more sharply than most.

Without work and feeling the hostility of neighbors who considered them part of the problem, many Mexicans opted for repatriation: They chose to go back to Mexico. Mexican workers in Tucson and the surrounding areas left by the thousands. In the Salt River valley alone, 6,400 Mexicans decided to repatriate in 1931. They joined more than 120,000 other returnees that year and a total of a half-million Mexican laborers who left the United States for Mexico between 1931 and 1935.[71]

Slowly, painfully, the local community was disintegrating. Mexicans and Americans polarized to an extent few had ever known. Suspicion and resentment grew as Mexicans drifted southward and Americans retreated into the comforting fantasy that the local community could function without half its number.

The Great Depression ended yet another episode in the border's history of progress and revealed latent tensions that compromised local relationships. Since the Treaty of Guadalupe Hidalgo artificially tore the region in two, alternating cycles of conflict and cooperation, boom and bust had kept life unsettled at best. None of these cycles, however, began along the border, among the people who either enjoyed or endured them. In every instance, national agendas and processes took precedence, driving changes both good and bad that altered the composition and character of the local community. The future of the border folk seemed destined to remain in hands other than their own.

By 1939, regional relations had become strained to the breaking point. The border economy was in a shambles; the community was polarized and adrift, pushed this way and that by outside forces. Then, war struck again. This time the fighting would take place thousands of miles away, on battlefields in Europe and the Pacific islands, and with far different consequences for the border's society, culture, and economy. A complete change in direction took place that ultimately led to a far more resilient local community. A border society that was capable of a greater degree of self-determination began to take form within Mexican and American nations that would come to be dependent on its energy, inventiveness, and diversity.

9

Braceros
to NAFTA,
1940–1994

The Treaty of Guadalupe Hidalgo ended a war and provided for peace, but the possibility of future hostilities along the international boundary was taken into consideration. The treaty's text included provisions to address the possibility of fighting breaking out once again. In fact, Article XXII dealt explicitly with how such a conflict might be contained in order to do the least damage to relations between Washington and Mexico City. The authors of the Treaty of Guadalupe Hidalgo, in other words, knew and sought to mitigate the bitter divisiveness and inherent destructiveness of war. It never entered their minds that war might actually draw Mexico and the United States closer together—not a war along the Rio Grande or in the deserts of Sonora, of course, but a global conflict half a world away.

World War II erupted on September 1, 1939, with the Nazi invasion of Poland. Within days, Great Britain and France declared war on Germany, and the greatest armed struggle in human history had begun. Not yet a combatant, the United States supported Great Britain with arms and supplies. Reluctantly at first, the nation prepared for entry into the campaign against Germany and its ally, Japan. Mexico had little interest in outright participation in the fighting, but informed observers could have easily foreseen an important role for the republic in the years ahead.

Unlike during World War I, the border remained at peace during the second conflict. There were no skirmishes, no hapless chases through the chaparral (a thicket of shrubs or small trees) in pursuit of elusive rebels, no Zimmerman Telegram to generate suspicion and enmity between Mexico and its neighbor. Indeed, the border region, far from being a trouble spot, became central to the American war effort and a force for progress in Mexico after the United States entered the fray in December 1941. The American side of the border came to play host to a vast industrial manufacturing complex, crucial military-scientific research facilities, and vital agricultural operations. Labor, or the shortage of it, became an issue. Hundreds of thousands of workers flocked to the American West and Southwest, but far more were needed. Mexicans once again satisfied that need, redefining Mexico's relationship with the United States and drawing the national centers into a new alliance.

The centerpiece of international cooperation was the Braceros Program, an effort to use Mexican hands to cultivate and harvest American crops. Launched in 1942, the joint project ran until 1964. During that time, large numbers of Mexican farm workers crossed the border to labor in fields growing food for the American market. These fields were located all along the border, but the largest share of migrant workers wound up in California. In fact, California absorbed half of the 219,000 Mexican farmhands who entered the United States between 1942 and 1947.[72] The state also claimed half of the irrigated land in the area: Of the 11,180,000 acres of irrigated fields in the border region by the end of the 1940s, 6,438,000 lay in California.[73]

Agriculture, however vital, represented only one aspect of an energized wartime economy that drew the border community out of the doldrums of the Great Depression. Beginning in 1943, farm workers were joined by tens of thousands of Mexican railway workers contracted by American railroad companies. In addition to the traditional commuter workers, who lived in Mexico but held jobs in the United States, the movement of industrial laborers and braceros represented perhaps the largest single international labor exchange in history and heralded a new age of Mexican-American interdependence. As one historian wrote, "This wartime flow of labor north to the U.S. border states and beyond marked the beginning of the massive influx of Mexicans to both the Mexican and U.S. border states."[74]

The border's people keenly felt the impact of international cooperation. Because of the migration of Mexicans who had decided on permanent relocation, the region's population became Mexican American perhaps more thoroughly then than at any time since the signing of the Treaty of Guadalupe Hidalgo. This was partly a function of sheer numbers. During the war years, the population of the American and Mexican border states surged upward. In 1940, the combined totals for residence on

During World War II, the U.S.-Mexico border region became central to the American war effort. One centerpiece of international cooperation was the Braceros Program which began in 1942 as an effort to use Mexican farm workers to help tend American crops. This Mexican migrant worker employed by the Braceros Program harvests tomatoes in California in 1961.

the U.S. side of the international boundary stood at 14,353,290; by 1950, these totals had grown to 19,728,191. The Mexican North experienced similar increases. The six states together claimed 13 percent (2,617,723) of Mexico's overall population in

1940. Ten years later, 15 percent (3,762,963) of Mexicans lived along the border.[75]

The region's economy expanded almost as rapidly as its population. Mexican exports in the 1940s ballooned. Minerals, cotton, and oil seeds led the way toward a Mexican gross domestic product that increased threefold over the next 20 years and sustained an annual growth rate of just over 6 percent. Investment in the Mexican North quadrupled, the amount of irrigated land rose in five of the six states, half of Mexico's total new roads were paved through the borderlands, and 60 percent of first-time Mexican bank loans went to Northern businesses.[76] Mexico boomed.

Across the line, the Americans made similar progress. California thrived on more than $35 billion in federal money allocated to that state between 1940 and 1946. The state's farms (on which so many Mexicans worked), its small and large businesses, and its industry used that windfall to drive an economy in which personal income topped $15 billion.[77] Although agriculture soaked up much of the available capital, industry took its share. Shipbuilding, aircraft assembly, steel milling, high technology, military research, and even military bases emerged as primary elements in California's general economy. In Arizona, New Mexico, and Texas, the story was much the same: breathtaking prosperity and a new economic infrastructure perfectly suited to the demands of the twentieth century.

By 1950, the border region enjoyed peace, renewed prosperity, and singular importance in the national economies of both the United States and Mexico. The border community regained its sense of place and collective identity. Cross-border interaction and interdependence rose to unprecedented levels and reminded border folk of the ties that traditionally bound them together—some of these ties bound them more tightly than others, but all bound them, just the same.

The reality of life along the border meant that the boundary line itself garnered little attention and certainly less respect from the local community than from the two national governments. As happened so often in the past, the inviolability of this fictional feature of the landscape occupied mental and ideological slots for the centers that simply did not exist for the periphery. The border community literally thrived on diversity, but the two republics, both Lázaro Cárdenas's Mexico and Franklin Roosevelt's United States, took pride in distinction. Eventually, the U.S. government, in particular, perceived a physical and cultural threat in what it viewed as a casual disregard for American sovereignty. The reemergence of what could only be construed as a bicultural border amplified the government's fears that the core concept of the nation itself was under attack. Equating each Mexican with one less American, the United States threw its power and authority behind an effort to militarize and thus secure "its" border against the Mexican "other."

The public expression of this novel, aggressive stance appeared in the mid-1950s. Operation Wetback represented the first wholesale government effort to rid the border states of Mexicans labeled "illegal." Spanning the years 1953–1955, the program deported 2 million Mexicans, mainly recent immigrants, but some citizens as well. An overly ambitious undertaking to begin with, Operation Wetback ultimately failed. The government could not fix the "problem" of local disregard for the border's presumed sanctity. Mexicans, in fact, entered the United States in even greater numbers, blending into a community that predated the boundary line and had already weathered similar waves of national interference in local processes.

The failure of Operation Wetback did not stop the central government in Washington from extending this military model during the late 1950s and 1960s. If anything, federal authorities became obsessed with border "security" as time went on, especially after the termination of the Braceros Program and the passage of stricter, more comprehensive immigration laws. Naive bids to fortify the line defied reality. The walls and fences that were eventually erected along the border protect Americans from a Mexican menace that existed solely in the popular imagination of groups that were either unable or unwilling to accept the complexity and diversity of the local community. Anti-immigrant and deportation campaigns, with revealing names such as Operation Gatekeeper (in California), Operation Safeguard (in Arizona), and Operation Hold the Line (in Texas) said more about the people who created them than those against whom they sought to defend the country. The photojournalist John Annerino, who accompanied undocumented Mexican workers as they risked their lives trying to enter the United States across the deserts of Arizona/Sonora, summed up matters by arguing that "nothing will stop these honest people in their quest for a better life, not the killing desert, and not the transformation of the 'tortilla curtain' into the Iron Curtain."[78] Indeed, the end result of such schemes is all too often the kind of violence that killed Esequiel Hernandez.

Local development, which characterized the postwar period, harmonized culture, society, and economy and produced an impetus toward future progress. This fact became apparent in the final third of the twentieth century. From 1960 to 1990, the populations of the four American and six Mexican border states doubled and in some cases nearly tripled. The total number of border inhabitants climbed from 33,091,165 to 65,173,819— evenly distributed on the Mexican side but concentrated in California and Texas on the American. California claimed more than half (57 percent) of the people who called the border home.

Perhaps of greater significance than the raw numbers of people involved in the expansion of the border community is where they lived. Between 1940 and 1990, the majority of border residents chose to live in cities. During World War II, the border community was split fairly evenly between those people living in rural areas and those living in cities. Fifty years later, 88 percent of border Americans lived in urban centers; 75 percent of Mexicans living along the border did likewise.[79] Even Americans and Mexicans moving into the region from other parts of their respective republics chose cities over small towns and farms. As a result of this phenomenon, paired matches of "sister cities" came to dominate the border. The blended metropolises that dot the international boundary function essentially as single entities, chopped into two by an arbitrary border. San Diego-Tijuana, Ciudad Juárez-El Paso, and Brownsville-Matamoros, among others, represent what Lawrence Herzog has called "a unique prototype of the human use of space: highly integrated, transfrontier metropolitan areas."[80] Like the rest of the border, these cities function as crossover points where the disparate Mexican and American realities flow into one fundamentally indivisible whole.

In human terms, urbanization helped the border achieve a higher level of bicultural integration. The local culture united art, architecture, language, food, entertainment, and even fashion into a single operative element. True, American and Mexican traditions influenced one another before 1848 and continued to do so throughout the nineteenth and twentieth centuries, but the process accelerated dramatically after World War II.

As one would expect, conflict still plagued social interaction along the borderline, but the local community generated its own unique modes of resolution, to a far greater extent than before. The border community has acted locally to resolve outstanding issues and to remedy shared problems from municipal sanitation to water use and pollution. Twin cities routinely act as if they constitute a single political unit. They acknowledge common urban needs and problems and seek out cooperative solutions that effectively erase the imaginary line that separates them. Law enforcement, fire protection, and health services are coordinated without reference either to the international boundary or the national governments that conceive of the border as some sort of firewall. The line divides Washington and Mexico City far more than it does transborder metropolises. As one El Paso–Ciudad Juárez resident put it, "The border [is] different from the rest of the country.... We're two joined cities and there has to be a certain *exchange* because we're united, because ... it's the same people."[81]

Between 1940 and 1990, both culturally and demographically, the border community developed what one observer referred to as nothing less than "the most complex bilateral relationship in the world."[82] A significant portion of this relationship was built around trade and cross-border commerce, much as the Treaty of Guadalupe Hidalgo had foreseen in 1848. The treaty envisaged an economic structure in which the United States and Mexico jointly exploited the border's potential to generate profit. Nicholas Trist and his Mexican counterparts, however, did not anticipate the explosive growth of the Díaz years, nor could they have imagined the *maquiladora* phenomenon, codified in the 1993 North American Free Trade Agreement (NAFTA), which, at least in economic terms, blotted out the line they had drawn at Guadalupe Hidalgo.

The maquiladora system, at first glance, resembles the old nineteenth-century structure arranged around Americans paying for Mexican labor to satisfy an essentially American consumer market. Money moves one way, and raw resources or finished goods move the other. What makes the maquiladoras different, however, is that they alter the traditional equation to provide much more extensive benefits to Mexico.

In the 1960s, American capital poured into sectors of the economy dealing with domestic market development, in terms of design and distribution. Manufacturing, on the other hand, shifted toward Mexico. The overall system that was slowly established functioned quite smoothly. Products for the American consumer market, created by vast sums of advertising dollars spent by American firms, were designed in the United States, with their components being either constructed at home or at least collected there from foreign sources. The parts were next shipped south to Mexico, assembled in maquiladora plants located within a few miles of the border, and then reshipped north for sale. American companies benefited from inexpensive Mexican labor, high levels of productivity, lower manufacturing outlays, and substantially lower operating cost. Companies received a bonus in the form of relaxed Mexican labor standards and often ill-enforced environmental laws. Mexican firms, in return, received much-needed capital investment that they used to modernize plant facilities and increase efficiency. Mexican workers enjoyed secure and, if not by American standards, high-paying jobs.

In 1965, a scant 12 border factories in Mexico churned out finished consumer goods for the U.S. market using American components. Within five years, 30 percent of all product parts sent outside the United States for assembly went to Mexico. By 1996, the number of maquiladora plants exceeded 2,000, employing nearly 650,000 Mexicans. These factories produced and shipped north a variety of goods, chief among them electronic components, TVs, toys, furniture, clothing, automobiles,

THE CHINA CHALLENGE

Mexico and the United States have shared a unique commercial relationship for more than 150 years. The basic combination of American capital and Mexican labor has gone through many changes over that time, yet most have been rather superficial. The essential character of the shared economy has remained remarkably fixed. Recently, however, a novel factor has been added to the equation—China. Traditionally, China served as a market for American goods, but in the last 10 years, the world's most populous country has repositioned itself to supplant Mexico as a source of low-cost labor and inexpensive consumer goods. In 1996, China increased its share of the export market in nearly every category, surpassing Mexico in the production and export of cameras, furniture, and computer equipment. In other areas, Mexico's lead is strong but far from secure. By 2002, Mexico's global competitiveness ranking fell below China's for the first time. As a result, hundreds of maquiladoras have closed their doors in the last few years. Hundreds of thousands of jobs have been lost, prompting the Mexican government to begin a frantic search for solutions. The obvious solution is one to which Mexico has turned for so long—the border itself. According to the economist Daniel H. Rosen, "Mexico's proximity to the U.S. market is the remaining hope."* The border and its economic potential, not to mention the border industry's ability to move goods into the United States quickly and at lowered transportation costs, may yet again prove to be the linchpin in U.S.-Mexican relations, as it was during the Díaz years and the Braceros Program.

* Rosen, "How China Is Eating Mexico's Lunch," p. 24.

and prepared foods. A renaissance in Mexican-American economic relations, focused on the border region, had become an indisputable fact by the early 1990s.

The North American Free Trade Agreement (NAFTA), passed by the U.S. Congress in November 1993, only accelerated a process well under way. In this, the trade agreement merely confirmed traditional border arrangements and took a step backward in time toward the Díaz years of "Order and Progress." The core of NAFTA, eliminating barriers to trade, seemed novel to the national governments in Washington and Mexico City, but more than one commentator noted that "the interdependence of the U.S. and Mexican economies had been a historical fact for at least a century," before the agreement went into effect.[83]

Under NAFTA, the border community flourished, but it had been doing that for a long time. Indeed, during the debates in Mexico over the agreement, manufacturers and merchants from the interior of the country, with the support of the central government, argued that duty-free imports would compromise their interests while enriching Mexican border businesses that dealt almost exclusively with American customers. Similarly, nonborder Americans claimed that jobs would be lost to Mexican workers who certainly would spend a large share of their income in the United States, but only along the border. The centers worried that the periphery might forget its place within the national schemes. In the end, NAFTA proved to be a qualified success, but, more important, the agreement emphasized what the border community already knew—the boundary line itself was utter fiction. Mexico and the United States had too much to gain from one another to let some map feature get in their way.

A single local community continued to thrive as a social and cultural meeting place, despite the creation of a supposedly unassailable border and despite walls and fences, armed clashes, deportation raids, and even shootings like the one that took place that spring day in Redford, Texas. As the new millennium dawned, the line inked onto a map in the town of Guadalupe

Hidalgo had begun to fade. That did not really matter, though; it had already become irrelevant as a force for separation. The border thus persisted as an imaginary artifact, shared and often quarreled over, but essentially the echo of a long-extinct worldview that assumed that somehow Mexicans and Americans could uncouple their common destinies. On a daily basis, people along the border prove how difficult it is to partition a community, to divide something that is inherently indivisible.

10

The Borderless Border

The Treaty of Guadalupe Hidalgo envisioned a clean and clear delineation between Mexico and the United States. The document assumed continued social and cultural contact and certainly foresaw economic exchanges along the border and beyond. Unfettered interaction of the kind that would today fall under the heading of globalization, however, was antithetical to the spirit of the treaty. Security against one's neighbor and gaining the international advantage served as its underlying objectives. Both of these imperatives required unequivocal division. If measured by this goal and in these terms, the treaty failed miserably.

Today, the border seems more like a dusty artifact of a bygone age than a functional point of reference one can use to understand what separates one country from another. Rather than a stark delineation, the boundary line serves more as a junction or, better, a convergence of disparate (very different) yet intimately related streams of cultural, social, and economic development. The central governments of the United States and Mexico, try though they might, cannot reverse the historical trends that have effectively dissolved the border.

Continued immigration, in both directions, mocks attempts to keep the border community neatly boxed up into north and south. Following established tradition, hundreds of thousands of Mexicans enter the United States each year, as legal, illegal, and temporary immigrants. Most of these people pick crops, work in light industry, and labor in the service sector, generating incalculable profits for American businesses and contributing large sums to local tax bases. The income the workers receive in return is sent back to Mexico in amounts great enough to affect the overall Mexican economy.

According to the *New York Times*, nearly 20 percent of all Mexican families receive money from members living in the United States. The total amount returned south of the border now stands at $14.5 billion, making this money the nation's second largest source of income after oil sales. By the year 2010, the total could top $25 billion, "a vast sum made of countless tiny payments by America's lowest-paid workers." For these men and women, like so many who came before them, the border is anything but a deterrent. Roberto Suro, an observer of Mexican-American relations and the director of the Pew Hispanic Center, has argued that no amount of border fortification or number of deportation raids would have dissuaded the more than 450,000 Mexican immigrants who entered the United States without papers last year. Suro contends that for "most Mexicans, the increased risks of crossing the border have had no impact on their willingness to migrate."[84]

International boundary or no, Mexicans continue to come. More than 200,000 Mexicans legally crossed the border in 2002 to take up permanent residence; another 118,835 entered the country as temporary workers. Substantial though these numbers are, they are dwarfed by the estimated 994,724 "deportable aliens," mostly from Mexico, detected by the U.S. Border Patrol living in the American Southwest.[85]

Many of the last group arrived in the United States after harrowing journeys across the blistering deserts of Arizona and Sonora. With the most convenient routes northward blocked by walls, fences, and militarized patrols, desperate immigrants set out on death-defying treks through a wilderness that is no less forbidding today than it was when the Treaty of Mesilla extended Guadalupe Hidalgo's imaginary line through it. Scalding heat, waterless wastes, and immense distances confront Mexicans determined to reach the United States. The results are often tragic. As John Annerino has revealed, the Arizona-Sonora desert is littered with the bones of the border's silent victims. From 1993 to 1996, 1,185 Mexicans died trying to cross the border; 28 percent of those unfortunate people died alone in the barren wastes where Sonora meets Arizona.[86]

The border flow, it should be remembered, is far from being one way. In small but growing numbers, Americans are moving southward, some for affordable housing and others in search of a Mexican lifestyle reputed to be less hurried and stressful than that common in the United States. Illegal American immigrants

In recent years, the U.S. Border Patrol has found nearly one million illegal immigrants from Mexico living in the American Southwest. Some Mexicans go to great lengths to cross the border, like this man who hid in the seat of a vehicle hoping to go unnoticed across the San Ysidro border in 2001.

aside, about 100,000 Americans currently live in Baja California alone. The Mexican town of San Felipe, just south of San Diego, is now home to just under 8,000 Americans, one-third of the town's total population. A bit farther north, 14,000 Americans live in the town of Rosarito. Across Mexico, American enclaves are being established in the form of housing developments aimed specifically at drawing new immigrants. More Americans—about 600,000 at last count, not including those living clandestinely as illegal immigrants[87] now live in Mexico than in any other foreign country.

Not only people cross the international boundary line as if it were not there; capital and goods do as well. Trade and commerce have never respected the border. That was true from the boom years of the nineteenth century to the Braceros period; it remains so today. The modern incarnation of this is the maquiladora. Notwithstanding recent stiff competition from China, Mexican factories remain central to the local economy and its larger national parent.[88] Plants along the border from Tamaulipas to Tijuana, where 69 percent of the maquiladoras are located, hum with activity. In 2002, while employing almost one million Mexicans, the maquiladoras purchased 97 percent of their components from the United States, at a total cost of $61 billion, which streamed north. All this money creates a reciprocal dependence that makes such things as borders seem quaint. The fact of Mexican-American economic cooperation is permanent and will continue to shape the future of a line that is relentlessly being erased by the constant back-and-forth movement of money and jobs.[89]

The border's future promises to be a continuation of its past in another important way: Conflict remains a vital element of the local experience and will probably be so in the decades to come. Beyond the actions of the national governments, which range from diplomatic disputes to the militarizing of the boundary, the local community endures bouts of anxiety and angry debate emerging from the process of cultural blending. Explosive and highly emotional issues periodically divide the local community. Among these, "English only" initiatives in the United States trigger bitter feuding over the essential character of an undeniably bicultural community. Perhaps no single aspect of culture defines a people as thoroughly as language. Whether the common tongue along the border will be Spanish, English, or some mix thereof (perhaps the hybrid language increasingly referred to as "Spanglish") is and will continue to be the subject of heated arguments.

A host of other matters falls into the same general cultural category as language. The debate over providing educational and social services to undocumented workers and their children is still simmering in California after it boiled over in the 1990s, resulting in the controversial ballot initiative known as Proposition 187. Although the measure failed under judicial review, being deemed too broad in what it denied to immigrants and a gross usurpation of federal powers by one state, Proposition 187 drew enough votes to pass in the popular balloting. The measure, denying education and health care to illegal aliens, pitted Californians against themselves and revealed the latent hostility that had been a part of border life since 1848.

Pollution, crime, and water use have all been points of contention at some time or another along the border. Local policymakers struggle to come up with cross-border remedies to these obstinate problems, but their voting publics cast blame north and south of the line at fellow community members. Americans demand stricter enforcement of existing Mexican environmental laws to halt the dumping of human and industrial waste into regional waterways and the ocean. Mexicans counter that their border neighbors want to stifle Mexican economic growth and lower the Mexican standard of living. Americans call for drug interdiction efforts by Mexican law-enforcement agencies; Mexicans remind the United States that the insatiable American market for illegal narcotics sustains the trade in the first place. Mexican and American farmers quarrel endlessly over scarce supplies of water, as do the municipal governments of border cities, each accusing the other of wastefulness and hoarding of a precious resource. Resource development, law enforcement, public services, education, health care, and even the words one speaks continually unite and divide the border folk, but they do so in a peculiarly local manner. In essence, the problems and solutions, the agreements and disagreements are all fundamentally local.

The national governments of the United States and Mexico are by no means bit players in this drama. The history of the border region demonstrates the power and influence the centers are capable of exerting over the periphery. For good or ill, Washington and Mexico City have the ability to alter border relations and change the way its people live. It is, in the end, *their* line anyway. Nevertheless, the U.S.-Mexican border is, as it always has been, a single place occupied by a complex community that in its daily reality is local, not national. The border's future, therefore, promises a continuation of the unique trajectory it has followed from the sixteenth century to today. A fully articulated community is still evolving along an arbitrary boundary line that blurs to the point of disappearing as one moves closer to it. The Treaty of Guadalupe Hidalgo divided the indivisible, bringing about more than a century and a half of struggle and controversy as well as progress and prosperity. From the Rio Grande to the California coast, a place and a people face the twenty-first century together.

1546   The discovery of silver near Zacatecas begins the process of settling the northern part of the Spanish empire in the New World.

1574   Fifteen hundred Spanish families begin forming a community along the Rio Grande River.

1776   California's initial colonization is completed with the establishment of a mission and presidio at what would become San Francisco.

1821   Mexico wins its independence from Spain; the first Americans are allowed to immigrate to Texas.

1853
Gadsden Treaty completes the U.S. acquisition of formerly Mexican territory

1574
Beginning of permanent settlements on the Rio Grande

1848
Treaty of Guadalupe Hidalgo is signed

1574   1853

1776
California is first colonized by Spain

1836
Texas rebels against Mexico's rule in the Texas Revolution

1836	Texas rebels against Mexican rule and becomes an independent state.
1845	Texas is annexed by the United States in July; it becomes a state in December.
1846–1847	The Mexican-American War is fought.
1848	American and Mexican delegates sign the Treaty of Guadalupe Hidalgo in February.
1853	The final part of the new U.S.-Mexican border is surveyed; James Gadsden negotiates the Treaty of Mesilla, giving the United States control of the area south of the Gila River.
1876–1910	The presidency of Porfirio Díaz ushers in decades of prosperity and progress along the border.
1910	The Mexican Revolution begins.

1910
The Mexican
Revolution begins

1940–1990
Braceros Program brings
Mexican workers to
the United States

1910

1997

1916
Pancho Villa's raid
on New Mexico
triggers U.S. intervention
in the Mexican Revolution

1997
Shooting of
Esequiel Hernandez
focuses media attention
on border tensions

1916	"Pancho" Villa's raid on Columbus, New Mexico, leads to the dispatch of an American force to hunt him down. Led by General John Pershing, the army of 6,000 pursues Villa for almost a year.
1920	Prohibition in the United States revives the border economy. The chief "products" are the entertainment and alcohol denied to Americans at home. Border cities thrive on the money and business brought to the region.
1929	The Great Depression brings the border revival to a halt and generates waves of American protectionism and Mexican repatriation.
1940–1990	The Braceros Program and the economic boom of World War II fundamentally alter the economy and demographics of the border region.
1965–1990	Maquiladora projects grow rapidly; border industry becomes vital to the Mexican and American economies during the 1990s.
1997	The shooting of Esequiel Hernandez focuses public media attention on the militarization of the U.S.-Mexico border.
2002	Competition from China threatens the resurgent border economy, which was based on maquiladora operations. The border enters a new stage in its evolution.

Chapter One

1. "Texas Town Still in Uproar Over Border Shooting," *CNNInteractive/CNN.com*, http://www.cnn.com/US/9708/15/border.shooting/, p. 1. Online. 8 October 2003.
2. "18-Year-Old Texan, Herding Goats, Killed by U.S. Marine Corps Anti-Drug Patrol; Criminal Investigation of Shooting Underway," *Friendly Fire (DRCNet Activist Guide)*, http://www.drcnet.org/guide8-97/friendlyfire.html, August 1997, p. 2. Online. 9 September 2003.
3. Ibid.
4. David E. Lorey, *The U.S.-Mexican Border in the Twentieth Century*. Wilmington, DE: SR Books, 1999, pp. 6, 8.
5. Lawrence A. Herzog, "Border Commuter Workers and the Transfrontier Structure along the *U.S.-Mexico Border*," in *U.S.-Mexico Borderlands: Historical and Contemporary Perspectives*, ed. Oscar J. Martinez. Wilmington, DE: SR Books, 1996, p. 178.
6. Pablo Vila, *Crossing Borders, Reinforcing Borders: Social Categories, Metaphors, and Narrative Identities on the U.S.-Mexico Frontier*. Austin: University of Texas Press, 2000, p. 9.
7. Herzog, "Border Commuter Workers," in Martinez, *U.S.-Mexico Borderlands*. 178.
8. "18-Year-Old Texan, Herding Goats, Killed by U.S. Marine Corps ...," p. 3.
9. Vila, *Crossing Borders*, p. 67.

Chapter Two

10. Paul Horgan, *Great River: The Rio Grande in North American History*. Hanover, NH: Wesleyan University Press, 1984, p. 7.
11. Patricia Nelson Limerick, *The Legacy of Conquest: The Unbroken Past of the American West*. New York: W. W. Norton, 1987, p. 228.
12. Lorey, *The U.S.-Mexican Border*, p. 8.
13. Ibid., pp. 18–20.
14. Thomas Torrans, *Forging the Tortilla Curtain: Cultural Drift and Change Along the United States-Mexico Border From the Spanish Era to the Present*. Fort Worth: Texas Christian University Press, 2000, p. 37.
15. Lorey, *The U.S.-Mexican Border*, p. 23.

Chapter Three

16. Horgan, *Great River*, p. 469.
17. Ibid., p. 509.
18. Ibid., p. 506.
19. Leonard Pitt, *The Decline of the Californios: A Social History of the Spanish-Speaking Californians, 1846–1890*. Berkeley: University of California Press, 1966, p. 6.
20. Ibid.
21. Ibid., p. 7.
22. Lorey, *The U.S.-Mexican Border*, p. 27.
23. Horgan, *Great River*, p. 514.
24. Ibid., pp. 520–521.

Chapter Four

25. Richard Griswold del Castillo, *The Treaty of Guadalupe Hidalgo: A Legacy of Conflict*. Norman: University of Oklahoma Press, 1990, p. 4.
26. Jerald A. Coombs, *The History of American Foreign Policy*. New York: Alfred A. Knopf, 1986, pp. 88–89.
27. Griswold, *Treaty*, p. 6.
28. Ronald Takaki, *A Different Mirror: A History of Multicultural America*. Boston: Little, Brown, 1993, p. 175.
29. Howard Zinn, *A People's History of the United States, 1492–Present*. New York: HarperCollins, 2003, p. 165.
30. Takaki, *A Different Mirror*, p. 175.
31. Zinn, *A People's History*, p. 164.
32. Pitt, *Decline*, p. 33.
33. Ibid., p. 29.
34. Ibid., pp. 29–30.

Chapter Five

35. Griswold, *Treaty*, pp. 183–184.
36. Ibid., p. 184.
37. Ibid., p. 187.
38. Ibid.
39. Ibid., p. 188.
40. Ibid.
41. Ibid.,
42. Ibid., pp. 189–190.
43. Roger Griswold del Castillo, "The Treaty of Guadalupe Hidalgo," in *U.S.-Mexico Borderlands*, p. 6.
44. Ibid.

Chapter Six

45. John Grassham, "The United States-Mexico Boundary Commission," in *The Treaty of Guadalupe Hidalgo, 1848: Papers of the Sesquicentennial Symposium, 1848–1998*, ed. John Porter Bloom. Las Cruces, NM: Doña Ana County Historical Society and Yucca Tree Press, 1999, p. 18.
46. Angel Moyano Pahissa, "The Mesilla Treaty, or Gadsden Purchase," in *U.S.-Mexico Borderlands*, p. 11.
47. "The Gadsden Treaty," in *U.S.-Mexico Borderlands*, p. 40.
48. Lorey, *The U.S.-Mexican Border*, p. 37.
49. Ibid., p. 37.
50. Ibid., p. 54.
51. Miguel Tinker Salas, "The Making of a Border Society, 1880–1910," in *U.S.-Mexico Borderlands*, p. 89.
52. Ibid., p. 90.

Chapter Seven

53. Lorey, *The U.S.-Mexican Border*, p. 59.
54. Griswold, *Treaty of Guadalupe Hidalgo*, p. 198.
55. Lorey, *The U.S.-Mexican Border*, p. 65.
56. Linda B. Hall and Don M. Coerver, "The Arizona-Sonora Border and the Mexican Revolution," in *U.S. Mexico Borderlands*, p. 119.
57. Ibid., p. 120.
58. Ibid., p. 121.
59. Ibid., p. 123.
60. Griswold, *Treaty of Guadalupe Hidalgo*, 197.
61. Ibid., p. 196.

Chapter Eight

62. Lorey, U.S. Mexican Border, pp. 69–70.
63. Ibid., p. 71.
64. Ibid., pp. 73.
65. Oscar J. Martínez, "Prohibition and Depression in Ciudad Juárez-El Paso," in *U.S.-Mexico Borderlands*, p. 152.
66. Ibid.
67. Ibid., pp. 153.
68. Ibid.
69. Ibid., pp. 154.
70. Ibid., pp. 156.
71. Thomas E. Sheridan, "*La Crisis*," in *U.S.-Mexico Borderlands*, p. 163.

Chapter Nine

72. Lorey, *The U.S.-Mexican Border*, p. 90.
73. Ibid., p. 88.
74. Ibid., p. 90.
75. Ibid., pp. 74, 118.
76. Ibid., pp, 86–87.
77. Ibid., pp. 85.
78. John Annerino, *Dead in Their Tracks: Crossing America's Desert Borderlands*. New York: Four Walls Eight Windows, 1999, p. 42.
79. Lorey, *The U.S.-Mexican Border*, pp. 124–125.
80. Herzog, "Border Commuter Workers," in *U.S.- Mexico Borderlands*, p. 186.
81. Vila, *Crossing Borders*, p. 64.
82. Bill Lenderking, "The U.S.-Mexican Border and NAFTA: Problem or Paradigm?" in *U.S.-Mexico Borderlands*, p. 194.
83. Lorey, *The U.S.-Mexican Border*, p. 170.

Chapter Ten

84. Ginger Thompson, "Money Sent Home by Mexicans Is Booming," *New York Times*, 28 October 2003: A12.
85. "Deportable Aliens Located by Program, Border Patrol Sector, and Investigations District: Fiscal Years 1993–2002," Table 40, *Yearbook of Immigration Statistics, 2002*, U.S. Citizenship and Immigration Services; www.bcis.gov/graphics/index.htm. Online. 27 October 2003.
86. Annerino, *Dead in Their Tracks*, p. 38.
87. Tim Weiner, "Americans Stake Claim in a Baja Land Rush," *New York Times*, October 26, 2003: A1.
88. See Daniel H. Rosen, "How China Is Eating Mexico's Lunch," *The International Economy* (Spring 2003): 22–25.
89. "Maquiladora History and Statistics," Mexico Maquiladora Manufacturing Information—Solunet: Infor-Mex., Inc.; http://www.solunet-infomex.com/faqs.html. Online. 29 October 2003.

Annerino, John. *Dead in Their Tracks: Crossing America's Desert Borderlands.* New York: Four Walls Eight Windows, 1999.

Barker, Malcolm E. *San Francisco Memoirs, 1835–1851: Eyewitness Accounts of the Birth of a City.* San Francisco: Londonborn Publications, 1994.

Combs, Jerald A. *The History of American Foreign Policy.* New York: Alfred A. Knopf, 1986.

"18-Year-Old Texan, Herding Goats, Killed by U.S. Marine Corps Anti-Drug Patrol; Criminal Investigation of Shooting Underway." *Friendly Fire (DRCNet Activist Guide).* http://www.drcnet.org/guide8-97/friendlyfire.html. Online. 27 September 2003.

Fox, Claire. *The Fence and the River: Culture and Politics at the U.S.-Mexico Border.* Minneapolis: University of Minnesota Press, 1999.

Griswold, Richard del Castillo. *The Treaty of Guadalupe Hidalgo: A Legacy of Conflict.* Norman: University of Oklahoma Press, 1990.

Horgan, Paul. *Great River: The Rio Grande in North American History.* Hanover, NH: Wesleyan University Press, 1984.

Institute for Public Strategies. "Law Enforcement to Crack Down on Youth Partying in Tijuana Over Labor Day Weekend." www.public-strategies.org. Online. 10 November 2003.

Limerick, Patricia Nelson. *The Legacy of Conquest: The Unbroken Past of the American West.* New York: W. W. Norton, 1987.

Lorey, David. *The U.S.-Mexican Border in the Twentieth Century.* Wilmington, DE: SR Books, 1999.

"Maquiladora History and Statistics." *Mexico Maquiladora Manufacturing Information-Solunet: Info-Mex., Inc.* http://www.sol-unet-infomex.com/faqs.html. Online. 29 October 2003.

Martínez, Oscar J, ed. *U.S.-Mexico Borderlands: Historical and Contemporary Perspectives.* Wilmington, DE: SR Books, 1996.

Morgan, Ted. *Wilderness at Dawn: The Settling of the North American Continent.* New York: Simon and Schuster, 1993.

111

"Partying in Matamoros, Mexico." http://www.maelstrom.org/mischief/history/mex.html. Online. 10 November 2003.

Pitt, Leonard. *The Decline of the Californios: A Social History of the Spanish-Speaking Californians, 1846–1890.* Berkeley: University of California Press, 1966.

Rosen, Daniel H. "How China Is Eating Mexico's Lunch." *The International Economy,* Spring 2003, 22–25.

Sadler, Louis R., ed. *The Treaty of Guadalupe Hidalgo, 1848: Papers of the Sesquicentennial Syposium, 1848–1998.* Las Cruces, NM: Dona Aña County Historical Society and Yucca Tree Press, 1999.

Takaki, Ronald. *A Different Mirror: A History of Multicultural America.* Boston: Little, Brown, 1993.

"Texas Town Still in Uproar Over Border Shooting." *CNN.com.* http://www.cnn.com/us/9708/15/border.shooting/. Online. 8 October 2003.

Thompson, Ginger. "Money Sent Home by Mexicans is Booming." *New York Times,* 28 October 2003, A12.

Torrans, Thomas. *Forging the Tortilla Curtain: Cultural Drift and Change Along the United States-Mexico Border From the Spanish Conquest to the Present.* Fort Worth: Texas Christian University Press, 2000.

U.S. Citizenship and Immigration Services. *Yearbook of Immigration Statistics, 2002.* http://uscis.gov/graphics/shared/aboutus/statistics/imm02yrbk/imm2002list.htm. Online. 27 October 2003.

Vila, Pablo. *Crossing Borders, Reinforcing Borders: Social Categories, Metaphors, and Narrative Identities on the U.S.-Mexico Frontier.* Austin: University of Texas Press, 2000.

Weiner, Tim. "Americans Stake Claims in Baja Land Rush." *New York Times,* October 26, 2003, A1.

Zinn, Howard. *A People's History of the United States, 1492–Present.* New York: Perennial Classics, 2001.

Cronon, William, George Miles, and Jay Gitlin, eds. *Under an Open Sky: Rethinking American's Western Past.* New York: W. W. Norton and Company, 1992.

Halevy, Drew Philip. *Threats of Intervention: U.S.-Mexican Relations, 1917–1923.* San Jose, CA: Writers Club Press, 2000.

Heizer, Robert F., and Alan F. Almquist. *The Other Californians: Prejudice and Discrimination Under Spain, Mexico, and the United States to 1920.* Berkeley: University of California Press, 1971.

Lamar, Howard, and Leonard Thompson, eds. *The Frontier in History: North America and Southern Africa Compared.* New Haven, CT: Yale University Press, 1981.

"The Militarization of the U.S.-Mexico Border," *In Motion Magazine.* http://www.inmotionmagazine.com/mj1.html. Online. 11 November 2003.

"U.S.-Mexico Border Issues," *Smithsonian Institution Libraries.* http://www.sil.si.edu/silpublications/us-mexico-border-issues.htm. Online. 11 November 2003.

"The U.S.-Mexico Border Resources Page." http://learning.berkeley.edu/Courses/AS102Sum97/resources.html. Online. 11 November 2003.

Utley, Robert M. *Changing Course: The International Boundary, United States and Mexico, 1848–1963.* Tucson, AZ: Southwest Parks and Monuments Association, 1996.

page:

John Davenport holds a Ph.D. from the University of Connecticut and currently teaches at Corte Madera School in Portola Valley, California. He lives in San Carlos, California, with his wife, Jennifer, and his two sons, William and Andrew.

George J. Mitchell served as chairman of the peace negotiations in Northern Ireland during the 1990s. Under his leadership, an historic accord, ending decades of conflict, was agreed to by the governments of Ireland and the United Kingdom and the political parties in Northern Ireland. In May 1998, the agreement was overwhelmingly endorsed by a referendum of the voters of Ireland, North and South. Senator Mitchell's leadership earned him worldwide praise and a Nobel Peace Prize nomination. He accepted his appointment to the U.S. Senate in 1980. After leaving the Senate, Senator Mitchell joined the Washington, D.C. law firm of Piper Rudnick, where he now practices law. Senator Mitchell's life and career have embodied a deep commitment to public service and he continues to be active in worldwide peace and disarmament efforts.

James I. Matray is professor of history and chair at California State University, Chico. He has published more than forty articles and book chapters on U.S.-Korean relations during and after World War II. Author of *The Reluctant Crusade: American Foreign Policy in Korea, 1941–1950 and Japan's Emergence as a Global Power*, his most recent publication is *East Asia and the United States: An Encyclopedia of Relations Since 1784.* Matray also is international columnist for the *Donga Ilbo* in South Korea.